The 4 Routes to Entrepreneurial Success

Contents

Acknowledgments

This book reflects the efforts and contributions of a great many people, and I want to thank these people both individually and collectively.

First and foremost are the hundreds of entrepreneurs and potential entrepreneurs who provided information of one kind or another to our research program. I want to express particular appreciation to those who agreed to have their case histories included in this volume. These case histories appear in Chapters 1 to 9, 11, and 13. The names indicated there are those of the actual entrepreneurs, and the firms are the ones in which they were involved.

Second, I owe thanks to the researchers with whom I worked. A project of this scope is not something that one can conduct alone. The cast of team members is set forth in Exhibit A1 in Appendix A. Among these, particularly important contributions came from Norman Smith, Fred Berman, John Oliver, Jeffrey Bracker, John O'del, Renato Bellu, Carol Newcomb, Eric Williams, and Juan Carlos Pastor. However, all 20 individuals deserve my appreciation for what they did.

I also want to thank three other people who have made this book possible. Steve Piersanti, president of Berrett-Koehler Publishers, not only gave me the support to see this project through to completion, but also contributed many useful ideas as well. Charlie Dorris was my developmental editor, but he was more than that, often introducing whole new ways of looking at a topic that I had only just barely glimpsed. Barb Miner, my wife, was my partner through many versions and rewrites. She not only put the manuscript into the computer again and again, but she made it better as well. Without these three people I might have had a manuscript, but there is considerable doubt whether I would have had a book that most people could understand.

INTRODUCTION

Four Types of Entrepreneurs, Four Ways to Succeed

Many people believe that there is an entrepreneurial personality—that certain kinds of people can struggle through to entrepreneurial success, whereas others cannot. And research supports this view. But why do some entrepreneurs fail in one venture only to succeed in another? Why do some entrepreneurs initially succeed in a venture but fail when their firm reaches a certain size? I have spent 20 years researching these and other questions about entrepreneurial success. During the last seven years of that research, I have studied 100 established entrepreneurs, using interviews, personality questionnaires, visits to their businesses, and lengthy discussions with them. I have also applied the same approach to over 150 students enrolled in an MBA-level entrepreneurship course.

Based on this research, I have developed a new view about entrepreneurs and why they succeed or fail.

- First, there is not a single type of entrepreneur, but rather, there are four different types, each with a distinct personality.
- Second, each type of entrepreneur must follow a distinct career route to succeed, and each must relate to the business in a different way.

This book discusses the four types of entrepreneurs, the route that each must take to be successful, and how to use this information to assess yourself or others.

If you are an entrepreneur, I want to help you recognize these entrepreneurial personalities in yourself and then show you how to use this knowledge to succeed.[1] If you are thinking about an entrepreneurial career, I want to help you identify whether you have entrepreneurial talents and the best way to use those talents. If you work with or for entrepreneurs, I want to help you better understand these entrepreneurs and create a mutually beneficial relationship with them. If you invest in entrepreneurial firms, either personally or through a banking or venture capital relationship, I want to help you make good investments.

Let me preview this book by briefly describing the research on which it is based, the four kinds of entrepreneurs, and how this book can be used.

RESEARCH

As I stated above, my research into entrepreneurship goes back 20 years. (Appendix A chronicles that research. And my use of "we" and "our" to describe the research reflects the many others with whom I have worked.) This book is primarily based on the part of the research begun in 1987. In that year the State University of New York at Buffalo (SUNY Buffalo) introduced a development program for established entrepreneurs and subsequently created an entrepreneurship course for MBA students. I was involved in those start-ups, and over the years they have provided a wealth of information about and insight into how entrepreneurs become successful. (Prior to 1987 we conducted a number of studies comparing entrepreneurs and managers, looking into high technology entrepreneurship, and studying entrepreneurs around the world.)

In the SUNY Buffalo development program, entrepreneurs made two-hour presentations to the class about their firms, and they completed 18 different measures designed to tap a wide range of personality characteristics.[2] With this information, I constructed a picture of how these people and their firms fit together, or in some instances did not fit. I spent considerable time reviewing these pictures with the participants.

When the program started, I decided to study 100 entrepreneurs in this manner; this would include a sufficiently wide range of personalities and firms on which to draw conclusions. I studied 10 to 20 individuals a year, reaching my goal in seven years. During this period, the MBA program at SUNY Buffalo introduced a course for students interested in starting a business after graduation. These students developed a plan for the type of venture they would like to create and also completed many of the questionnaires that the established entrepreneurs had filled out. In a five-year period, more than 150 students took the course, thus adding firsthand information about how entrepreneurs think before starting their venture—information not available from the established entrepreneurs.

We followed the progress of both the entrepreneurs and the students after they left the course. For the entrepreneurs, we interviewed them at their businesses. For the students, who were much more widely dispersed, we corresponded with letters and telephone calls to establish who had started a business and of what kind.

From this work have come my insights into what it takes to become a successful entrepreneur. But these insights have not come quickly or easily. I made many comparisons between scores on the questionnaires and information on individuals and firms, including such measures of success as annual dollar volume of sales, net profit on sales, and the number of employees. A large volume of computer processing and statistical analysis was involved.

However, some of the best insights have come from talking to and working with the entrepreneurs and the students. I spent many hours with students considering possible ventures. We discussed feasibility and sources of capital, but we also talked about personality patterns and how the business might be structured to fit their needs. The discussions with established entrepreneurs were even more helpful. In some cases, these extended over many hours, occurring at social events and at chance meetings as well as in our offices. During this period I worked with a number of entrepreneurial firms in Western New York in consulting relationships, trying to help them grow more effectively. These relationships, too, provided a wealth of information.

A few of these discussions and relationships had a particular influence on my thinking—a recovered alcoholic whom I helped find new meaning in his business; a father-son conflict over succession, which placed me on a board of directors slate; two brothers who were left a business on their father's death and needed to sort out their relationships in it; an entrepreneur who had never planned anything in his life and wanted to plan his disengagement from one line of business and entry into another; two partners in a rapidly growing venture who wanted assistance in looking at the ways their personalities might fit together in a much larger business; the several cases where the fit with an entrepreneurial career was not good and an alternative had to be found; a woman whose husband was dragging the business down; a top-notch salesperson entrepreneur who needed help finding a general manager.

These kinds of situations really got me thinking, in part because of the specific problem at hand, but also because they represented gateways to solving larger problems involving the career success of a whole group of entrepreneurs. Ideas would come out of particular relationships with entrepreneurs who had problems. To see if the ideas were valid, I would go to the mass of information we had about established entrepreneurs and future entrepreneurs. If my ideas fit the data, they became candidates for this book.

This extensive research provides the basis for my ideas about the four types of entrepreneurs.

THE FOUR TYPES OF ENTREPRENEURS

Four types of entrepreneurial personalities exist:

1. The Personal Achiever
2. The Supersalesperson
3. The Real Manager
4. The Expert Idea Generator

The Personal Achiever

People who need to achieve have a good chance of becoming successful entrepreneurs.[3] However, entrepreneurial success is not merely a matter of wanting or needing to achieve.

Personal Achievers are classic entrepreneurs, bringing tremendous energy to their companies and putting in long hours at work. They like feedback about their performance, and they like to plan, including setting goals for future achievements. They have a lot of initiative and a strong commitment to their organizations. Personal Achievers believe that they control their lives through their own actions rather than being controlled by circumstances or the actions of others. And for Personal Achievers work should be guided by their own goals (not someone else's).

Personal Achievers are most likely to succeed if they pursue the Achieving Route: constantly putting out fires and dealing with crises, wearing many hats depending on which crisis is paramount at the moment, and trying to be good at everything.

The Supersalesperson

Supersalespeople possess a great deal of feeling for other people and want to help them in any way possible. Supersalespeople use a soft-sell approach, and they receive sales from their customers' desire to give something back. Relationships are very important to them, and they like social situations and groups. They consider selling to be essential to their companies.

To succeed as entrepreneurs, Supersalespeople need to use the Selling Route: spending as much time as possible selling and getting someone else to manage the business.

The Real Manager

Real Managers like to take charge; they do well in corporate leadership positions; they are competitive, decisive, and positively disposed to those with authority; they enjoy power and acting a part. Often they come to entrepreneurship from larger firms. As entrepreneurs, they frequently become effective marketers, partly by managing the marketing process but often by being good salespeople. They manage customers into a sale—by using logic and forceful persuasion. Thus their approach is quite different from that of the Supersalesperson.

Their strength is managing ventures into major growth. They do not need a general manager; they are the general manager. Their ideal path to success is the Managing Route: finding or starting a business large enough to need their managerial talents.

The Expert Idea Generator

Expert Idea Generators invent new products, find new niches, develop new processes, and generally find a way to outthink the competition. These are innovators in the true entrepreneurial sense. They are strongly drawn to the world of ideas. Yet they can get carried away by their enthusiasms and fail to take sufficiently calculated risks; to mitigate the risks of unwarranted enthusiasm, a degree of cautiousness helps here. Also, on occasion, they can be somewhat idealistic.

Their ideal route to entrepreneurial success is the Idea Generating Route: to think their way through situations, to be visionaries for their firms. They are often involved in high technology venturing.

These four personality patterns are quite diverse. Some successful entrepreneurs have only one of the four patterns; some have several. The key: If you have a given pattern, success comes only if you find situations in which you can use your strengths. For example, if you are a Supersalesperson, do not spend most of your time at a desk performing administration. To be successful, the entrepreneur's personality and behavior must fit together.

In addition to playing to your strengths, however, you must cover for your weaknesses. If you are a Supersalesperson bringing in new business, your firm must still be managed. If you are an Expert Idea Generator creating new ideas, your firm needs a system to get them to market. This is a complex matter, and two chapters are devoted to each type of entrepreneur and how each achieves success. I hope to help you learn the four patterns well enough to easily identify them in yourself or in others. As part of the process, I will frequently illustrate points using case studies of established entrepreneurs from the group of 100 identified by their real names and actual firms. These case examples appear in Chapters 1 to 9, 11, and 13.

Appendix B describes my procedure for identifying the four types of entrepreneurs. The material is somewhat technical, but I believe that it will help you understand the four patterns. Appendix B also notes publications that provide more information about these procedures. The reference section that follows Appendix B provides detailed citations for publications mentioned in the Notes at the end of chapters and also in the appendixes.

WHO SHOULD READ THIS BOOK

If people fully understand the four patterns that my research identifies, and the kinds of behavior that each requires, they can use this knowledge to great personal advantage.

Established entrepreneurs can assess their own talents.

- Successful entrepreneurs can obtain a new perspective on current problems and how to solve them, and on likely pitfalls and how to avoid them.
- Failed entrepreneurs can gain insight into their past mistakes and find ways to succeed next time.

Prospective entrepreneurs can also assess their own talents.

- Anyone who is considering some type of start-up or business purchase can assess their chances of success.
- Those who have experienced a corporate layoff and are considering a new career in entrepreneurship can better appreciate the likelihood of success and how they should approach such a career.
- Members of a new generation who are considering entering a family business, or who have already done so, can better judge their choice and their role in the business.
- Venture managers, and those who face the prospect of becoming venture managers, can determine whether that path is for them and, if so, how they should follow it.

People can assess the entrepreneurs with whom they are working or thinking about working.

- Senior managers and human resource managers can more appropriately staff corporate ventures.
- Bankers, venture capitalists, economic development agency managers, and other investors can better assess the risk and return related to their investment.

- Judges handling bankruptcy proceedings can determine the feasibility of successful reorganizations.
- Employees of an entrepreneurial venture can understand the entrepreneur and thus work more effectively with him or her and make better judgments about the firm's future.
- Entrepreneurs who are considering joining a business partnership can determine whether it will work, whether any particular partner is unsuited for the venture, and how the business should be structured to capitalize on the special talents of each partner.
- Owners of family businesses who are uncertain about turning the business over to a new generation can assess their potential successors and thus make more informed decisions regarding succession issues.

CONCLUSION

The first part of this book—Chapters 1 to 9—discusses the four types of entrepreneurs and their routes to success, and those people who have more than one entrepreneurial pattern (complex entrepreneurs). The remainder of the book shows you how to use this knowledge in more specific respects:

Chapter 10—How to apply my personality patterns to assess yourself and others.

Chapter 11—How well women and men compare as to the four entrepreneurial types and their appropriate routes.

Chapter 12—The value of entrepreneurial development programs and of formal degree programs, and the things to look for in these programs.

Chapter 13—The career route to take if you do not fit into any of the four categories of entrepreneurs and still wish to experience a degree of entrepreneurship.

NOTES

1. Ann G. Ehringer emphasizes the importance of this awareness of self in her book *Make Up Your Mind*. She calls it awareness of mind, which for entrepreneurs means understanding the process of your thinking, under-

standing the patterns of your decision making, and understanding your personal principles. She provides numerous examples of how this kind of self-understanding contributes to entrepreneurial success.

2. Appendix B provides detailed information on these measures and on how they are used to develop entrepreneurial types.

3. Much of the early evidence on this point is contained in the book *The Achieving Society* by David C. McClelland.

CHAPTER 1

The Personal Achiever
Entrepreneur

Personal Achievers are the classic entrepreneurs, the people we usually picture when thinking about an entrepreneur. This chapter describes them—their characteristics, their working styles—and uses case studies to illustrate what a successful Personal Achiever looks like. The next chapter discusses the career route that Personal Achievers must take to be successful entrepreneurs.

WHAT MAKES A PERSONAL ACHIEVER

Personal Achievers possess seven interconnected characteristics, all directly related to entrepreneurial success.[1] Some of these characteristics are unique to successful entrepreneurship, others may be found in people who succeed in other fields. And the exact mix of these characteristics varies among Personal Achievers. Nevertheless, those who have a majority of these characteristics are Personal Achievers and should become entrepreneurs.

Of the four types of entrepreneurs, Personal Achievers are the only type who really must become entrepreneurs to succeed; in other settings, they may fail.

The characteristics of Personal Achievers are as follows:

1. Need to achieve
2. Desire for feedback
3. Desire to plan and set goals
4. Strong personal initiative

5. Strong personal commitment to their organization
6. Belief that one person can make a difference
7. Belief that work should be guided by personal goals, not those of others

Need to Achieve

Because achievement is a major source of satisfaction to Personal Achievers, they are more concerned with achieving success than with avoiding failure. Personal Achievers carefully analyze the probabilities for the success of different alternatives. And, to ensure that any success can be attributed to their own efforts, they prefer alternatives with clear-cut, individual responsibility. This need to achieve produces several effects in a Personal Achiever.

Personal Achievers are usually highly rational decision makers. They could make good corporate managers; however, their strong need for individual credit can make it difficult for them to cooperate fully with others. Yet in an entrepreneurial situation, they can invest huge amounts of energy to make a firm succeed.

As entrepreneurs, many Personal Achievers become workaholics and overload themselves. Yet by working long hours, they often accomplish more, thus besting less driven competitors. This is particularly important in the early stages of an entrepreneurial venture when employees are few, and the Personal Achiever's long hours can keep costs down without hurting productivity.

Along with working long hours, Personal Achievers are hard-driving and competitive, constantly struggling to accomplish more and more in less and less time. Thus, they hate being idle and have a chronic sense of time pressure; they are often somewhat hostile and impatient with people and situations that seem to block accomplishments, which may place them in conflict with the opposing efforts of others.[2]

With their work habits, Personal Achievers are under great stress, stress that they may hold in and take home at night. They thus have more time to work; they are solving problems, not just worrying. But although being driven helps them to succeed, it may exact a price: a greater tendency to heart disease.[3] Yet I have not found any particularly marked incidence of heart problems among Personal Achievers I have studied. Perhaps being driven creates fewer health problems if people are true to themselves and win at the same time.

The other price that Personal Achievers may pay: less meaningful family time. The family may fail, even as the venture succeeds. But according to my findings, the pluses outweigh the minuses for Personal Achievers. They will work very hard and devote little time to their families in any event, unless they induce family members to work with them in the business. Among the Personal Achievers with whom I have worked, family problems, and even divorce, are frequent. On the plus side, the gratification from achievement satisfies strong needs, and this more than offsets the minus of family problems. As will be discussed in Chapter 2, when conflicts occur between Personal Achievers and their families, it is the families that probably must adjust the most.

Desire for Feedback

Personal Achievers need feedback about whether they are succeeding or failing. Feedback about profitability, productivity, breakage, accounts receivable, inventory turnover, and the like becomes an important way for them to attribute any success in the venture to their own efforts. Annual dollar volume of sales is particularly important. Feedback of this kind keeps a Personal Achiever's batteries charged and the energy flowing.

Desire to Plan and Set Goals

Personal Achievers think about the future and are energized by the prospects of future achievements. Consequently, they approach their work with a strong focus on future possibilities, rather than a preoccupation with current problems. They like to plan, to set personal goals that will signify personal achievement, and to plot paths to those goals. Implicit in this process is a minimal expectation, or fear, of true failure. A strong desire to plan and set goals for future achievements can get these people through the rough spots more easily. Personal Achievers work very hard because they know there is gold at the end of the rainbow, and they have figured out how to get there.

Strong Personal Initiative

Personal Achievers show great initiative; they act independently and initiate action without any stimulation or support from others.[4] Personal Achievers do not require a superior or coworkers to initiate things or support them; that would detract from their sense of personal accomplishment and worth. They are self-starters, and they want to be able to say "I did it myself." Being the initiator may mean working harder and longer, but it satisfies more, simply because there is no need to share the credit for starting a course of action.

Strong Personal Commitment to Their Organization

Personal Achievers are fiercely committed to their organization. They believe strongly in its goals and values, they are willing to work hard for the organization, and they want to belong to the organization for a long time.[5]

Personal Achievers identify with their ventures much as doctors or lawyers identify with their professions. Perhaps even more so. I have heard many Personal Achievers speak of their venture as if it were a baby to which they had given birth. They will do anything to keep the venture alive and well, and to nurture it into a success. Such commitment can bring heartbreak if the venture and the entrepreneur separate. Some Personal Achievers do sell their ventures voluntarily, but in my experience, that happens only after considerable pressure from business circumstances. Those who buy and sell several companies may not feel quite this same sense of commitment to each venture. Yet the first sale of a business is likely to be a wrenching experience even for these people.

And as for retirement, Personal Achievers loath it, often continuing to work at their firms well into their 70s and even 80s. They may in fact refuse to let go, relinquishing the reins only when a board of directors or legal action requires it.[6] The tenacity with which Personal Achievers hold onto their firms and their work absolutely amazes me.

This commitment also underlies a desire to find out information about the venture, information to help it survive and prosper. This is not the scholarly dedication of the intellectual, nor is it a love of learning for its own sake. It is a practical desire to acquire any information that will make the venture more successful—technical knowledge, knowledge of business management, competitor intelligence, or anything else that promises to contribute. Personal Achievers will master some new subject, even though were it not for the business they would have absolutely no interest in the topic. Their dedication to practical learning far exceeds what one finds in the normal classroom; they are a pleasure to teach (as long as one teaches them the "right things").

Belief That One Person Can Make a Difference

Personal Achievers believe that they control their lives, rather than being controlled by another person or by something else beyond their influence. (They have an "internal locus of control.") They plan actions and work hard to achieve goals because trying hard is likely to pay off, because what one does personally can make a difference.

On the other hand, people with an "external locus of control" believe that their fate lies with persons and circumstances beyond their control (with people in positions of power such as bosses or government officials, or with chance factors such as luck). These people are unlikely to work hard; the work may be a waste of time. Beliefs like these strangle the drive to achieve, to take personal initiative, to plan, and to commit strongly to the organization, drives that characterize a Personal Achiever's approach to life.

Belief That Work Should Be Guided by Personal Goals, Not Those of Others

Personal Achievers are individualistic; in an ideal world, they would prefer to work free from superiors who tell them what to do, professional organizations that set ideal standards for their performance, and peer groups that constrain their actions. Many Personal Achievers find this freedom in their ventures. They believe a really good job is one where people set their own goals, strive to accomplish these goals as they see fit, and live or die by their ability to plan and achieve results. To the extent a job departs from this ideal, it is somewhat personally demeaning. Furthermore, people and things that intrude, and thus restrict personal freedom, are strongly resented; such may be the fate of government agencies, bank loan officers, labor unions, overly demanding venture capitalists, and the officers of corporations that spawn new ventures.

In particular, Personal Achievers tend to avoid participation in group activities that might pressure them into actions or make decisions for them. In an ideal work situation, it is possible to identify who did the work and who should get the credit. To the extent group processes interfere with this, they are to be avoided. Participative approaches, group decision making, and employee empowerment may be fine for others, but not for Personal Achievers.

As a by-product of this individualistic approach, Personal Achievers prefer not to have partners, and to get rid of them as quickly as possible.[7] Personal Achievers do not enjoy operating in a peer group context, even a group of two. Thus they will suffer partners only when the benefits substantially outnumber the costs. And even then it is difficult.

You may recognize these characteristics in yourself or in someone you know. But remember, any single Personal Achiever may exhibit all seven of the characteristics, but more typically several will be missing.

WHAT PERSONAL ACHIEVERS LOOK LIKE

Like pieces in a jigsaw puzzle, each of the seven characteristics discussed above shows a part of the Personal Achiever. Let's now look at the Personal Achiever as a whole.

Personal Achievers are occasionally called "quarterbacks."[8] In the early stage of a venture, structuring the work and the organization is not important. Success comes from energy, commitment, confidence, esprit de corps, and a belief that too much structuring would be harmful. Leaders, as quarterbacks, are active "doers," handling crises and constantly putting out fires, operating as team leaders more than managers. Later they become recruiters, schedulers, budgeters, and anything else the venture may require. Managing in the usual sense is only a small part of this process. Many things must be done, few people are there to do them, and even fewer who have any real knowledge in an area. The Personal Achiever thus becomes a company expert on many things simply because someone has to learn how to handle them. (People learn quickly under these circumstances.)

But through it all, the Personal Achiever, like a quarterback, wants to make a first down, and then another, and ultimately to score. For Personal Achievers, however, scoring and winning are not a matter of field goals and touchdowns, but of dollar sales volume, number of employees, and profit margins. Personal Achievers are generalists in the true sense of the word, but they are not necessarily general managers. More often, they are general doers. They wear many hats, changing them constantly.

To make the picture of the Personal Achiever more specific, look at two case studies: Jacqueline Taylor of Stovroff and Taylor Travel, and Richard Pohlman of the Pohlman Foundry Company.

Jacqueline Taylor of Stovroff and Taylor Travel

Stovroff and Taylor is a relatively new travel agency owned 50-50 by two women who spent most of their prior careers together in the real estate business. After selling that business, they formed the travel agency, even though neither had previous experience in the field. It is a female/minority-owned company, and that status is used to advantage. Some 90 percent of the business is corporate in nature; the remainder is leisure. Although most clients are located in the greater Buffalo area, some business is in other parts of the country.

The agency has grown rapidly and is now at $15 million in annual billings. There are 36 employees. As with most full-service travel agencies, profit margins are rather thin. In fact, sales began to approximate the $10 million figure before profitability was attained. However, the business has made a profit for several years now.

Taylor is primarily a Personal Achiever, secondarily a Supersalesperson, and she has some of the Real Manager in her as well. But it is the Personal Achiever pattern that is most manifest in her behavior within the company. She loves to grow organizations and receive feedback on how well she is doing along the way. Dedicating her energies to this kind of achievement is extremely attractive to her, but planning in any detail how to get to where she is going is another matter. She is primarily an action person who believes her actions are what make things happen. There is good reason to work hard because her hard work will pay off in satisfying personal accomplishments. There is a good deal of tension and stress in all this. Deadlines must be met, problems cannot be left unresolved, and perfection needs to be at least approximated if not always fully achieved.

Taylor remains in high gear even when she is away from work. Learning new things comes easily to her and she fully enjoys seeking out what she needs to know to do her work better. The company she has formed and grown is very important to her, and she is willing to devote a great deal of time and energy to it. She likes making her own decisions at work, and Stovroff and Taylor is the perfect vehicle for that purpose.

As is typical of Personal Achievers, she scores high on many characteristics, but not all.

Need to achieve	*Very High*[9]
Desire for feedback	*Very High*
Desire to plan and set goals	*Not a Factor*
Strong personal initiative	*Not a Factor*
Strong personal commitment to their organization	*Very High*
Belief that one person can make a difference	*High*
Belief that work should be guided by personal goals, not those of others	*High*

Taylor and her partner divide their work in a way that gives Taylor primary responsibility for all inside operations, with the title of executive vice president. Thus she handles such matters as vendor relations, salaries, and preparation and presentation of proposals to clients, and she works closely with the accounting department. Only the outside account executives are assigned to her partner. Corporate agents, leisure business, quality control, packaging, and delivery all require her supervision. She sells to a number of corporate clients personally. To handle all this she typically puts in seven days a week at the office. She is best described as a crisis manager who deals with problems as they arise. Somehow there never has been time to develop a business plan or a budget.

The partners retained a widely respected consultant in the industry to teach them the travel business. This arrangement continued for several years until they felt they had absorbed sufficient information to go on their own. At several points it has seemed appropriate to open branch locations, and this has been done. It has not always worked out well. Thus there have been several openings and closings. As the business grows, there is more demand for the agency to put together organized tours and do meeting planning. There seems always to be something new to handle. Yet Taylor really enjoys the hectic pace, and the fact that the company continues to surpass other travel agencies in the area as it grows provides her with considerable satisfaction.

Richard Pohlman of Pohlman Foundry Company

Pohlman Foundry is a century-old jobbing foundry producing gray and ductile iron castings manufactured to customer specifications and weighing anywhere from less than a pound to over 10,000 pounds. The premachined castings are used as parts for pumps, compressors, turbines, refrigeration units, machine tools, and punch product equipment. They are often difficult and complex to produce and yield a premium price for their very high quality. Exploiting this niche, the company is able to survive where others have not. It is one of the few such companies remaining in New York State from what at one time was a sizable industry.

The stock of the company is all owned by members of the Pohlman family, no one of whom has a majority interest. In recent years the number of employees has trended downward from a peak of 150. Sales were running at the $7.5 million level until the recession, when they dropped by about $1 million. Overall the company is profitable even while paying down its debt, but again the recession has had an impact.

Richard Pohlman now runs the company with the title of president, but he has been with it in various other capacities for over 20 years. He is the only third-generation family member currently active in the firm. Previously he was an FBI agent, having earned a law degree from the State University of New York at Buffalo.

Pohlman has the characteristics of a good salesperson, and in fact does spend a good deal of time with customers. This quality also proves valuable in dealing with the vicissitudes of a family-operated business, where no one has a controlling interest. However, it is the high level of energy he invests in everything he does (his Personal Achiever qualities) that stands out. Like so many people of this type, Pohlman is strongly motivated by a desire for personal achievement. He likes to be associated with a successful enterprise and to feel that he is contributing substantially to that success. He wants to obtain feedback so he can determine how well he is doing; in short, he seeks some means of keeping score. He tends to establish goals for future accomplishment and to plan how the company can achieve those goals.

Knowledge is important to him; it helps him plan. Being a professional, an attorney, this is not surprising, but this search for learning extends into many areas of the business that have little if anything to do with legal matters. Pohlman is the kind of person who becomes strongly committed to activities and organizations—his profession yes, but also the company for which he feels a strong sense of personal responsibility. He has considerable discretion to do things his own way, yet at the same time he is bound by the traditions of a firm that now employs members of the fourth generation of the owning family. His vision for the company may on occasion outdistance what it is possible to do in this context. When he has more tenure as president, however, the situation may change.

These characteristics are exhibited in the test pattern as follows:

Need to achieve	*Very High*
Desire for feedback	*Very High*
Desire to plan and set goals	*High*
Strong personal initiative	*Not a Factor*
Strong personal commitment to their organization	*Very High*
Belief that one person can make a difference	*Not a Factor*
Belief that work should be guided by personal goals, not those of others	*Very High*

Pohlman is in fact involved in every aspect of the business—costing, budgeting, union negotiations, sales, marketing, legal, and anything else that appears to require his attention. He is actively trying to bring along young non–family members to manage many aspects of the business. He has worked with the technology since his employment as a molder and coremaker during high school, and he continues to keep on top of new developments. Major areas that he is overseeing include development of the management organization, with an emphasis on team building; completion of conversion to a management information system (MIS); the full utilization of an Alpha set no bake binder system; the installation of a total quality management program with the goal of certification as an ISO-9002 supplier; replacement and upgrading of capital equipment as required; and review and replacement of current processes, materials, and methods where technological improvements seem to warrant it. He is trying to find a way to obtain growth capital, perhaps through some type of refinancing, and to deal with problems created by the New York State Department of Environmental Conservation with regard to solid waste disposal emanating from excess sand generated in the production process.

On top of all this, he has operated a corporate legal practice in his free time for many years. This is primarily a labor of love. Pohlman is without question a very busy man.

CONCLUSION

Personal Achievers are the classic entrepreneurs, and only as entrepreneurs can they fully utilize their talents and achieve real success.

Personal Achievers can do other things, especially if they show any of the other entrepreneurial personality patterns: Supersalesperson, Real Manager, or Expert Idea Generator. And Personal Achievers can perform well as corporate managers, but only if that work provides them with the experience to subsequently become an entrepreneur. Ultimately, they tend to run afoul of the large corporation, not because they necessarily have problems with authority but because they want to follow their own path. Often Personal Achievers become entrepreneurs because an employer will not do something that they are absolutely sure will work. Yet just as often, they become entrepreneurs at an early age, convinced that no one else can do a particular job as well as they.

Personal Achievers can be recognized by their characteristics:

1. Need to achieve
2. Desire for feedback
3. Desire to plan and set goals
4. Strong personal initiative

5. Strong personal commitment to their organization
6. Belief that one person can make a difference
7. Belief that work should be guided by personal goals, not those of others

Most Personal Achievers will have a majority of these characteristics, so while not identical, Personal Achievers are similar—a similarity that allows them to succeed using the Achieving Route, discussed in the next chapter.

NOTES

1. The evidence for this is considered at length in a book titled *Entrepreneurial Behavior* by Barbara J. Bird.
2. This in many respects reflects the Type A personality described by Michael T. Matteson and John M. Ivancevich in their book *Managing Job Stress and Health*.
3. This link is explored extensively in a book by Michael J. Strube titled *Type A Behavior*.
4. Initiative of this kind is discussed by Edwin E. Ghiselli in *Explorations in Managerial Talent*.
5. A great deal of information related to these factors can be found in *Employee-Organization Linkages: The Psychology of Commitment, Absenteeism, and Turnover* by Richard T. Mowday, Lyman W. Porter, and Richard M. Steers.
6. Jeffrey Sonnenfeld in his book *The Hero's Farewell* provides a good description of this refusal to let go.
7. This process is well described by Orvis F. Collins and David G. Moore in their classic study *The Enterprising Man*, which also provides a good portrait of how the careers of Personal Achiever entrepreneurs evolve.
8. Jay Galbraith discusses this idea in his article on the topic in the *Journal of Business Strategy*.
9. In this and all following cases, "Very High" means very much characteristic and equals a pattern score of 2 in Appendix B; "High" means characteristic to a sizable degree and equals a pattern score of 1 in Appendix B; and "Not a Factor" means less characteristic and equals a pattern score of 0 in Appendix B.

CHAPTER 2

How Personal Achievers Succeed or Fail

Chapter 1 discussed the seven characteristics of Personal Achievers. But to succeed, Personal Achievers must be able to fully use these characteristics and must be in the right environment, which for them means following the Achieving Route. Like any journey, taking the Achieving Route requires understanding what it is, how and where to start, and how to avoid the traps that lead to failure. These are the subjects of this chapter.

THE ACHIEVING ROUTE

The Achieving Route requires Personal Achievers to be themselves:

1. Be Energetic—Devote your very substantial energies as fully as possible to the venture, throwing yourself into the work and spending long hours at it. Believe in yourself and in what you are doing.
2. Learn—Learn all you can about the business. But do not limit this learning to the business as it is today. Learn things that will be needed in the future as well. Have a vision of what the venture will become, picture the things you will need to know when the vision materializes, and learn them.
3. Plan—Implied in this need to learn is the need to plan. Personal Achievers find it natural to think about the future and what they will achieve. But go beyond the dreams to more systematic planning. Write down specific goals that will really tax you. Establish timetables for getting to your goals and procedures for reaching them. This

is not something to do and then put away in a drawer; do it on a continuing basis, constantly revising, as new problems are faced and new things are learned.

4. Be Flexible—Keep your venture as unstructured and free-form as possible when it is small. A little business is like a piece of wood floating down a river. To keep from getting hung up on every rock and jetty, it must respond rapidly to changing currents. Personal Achievers can be flexible and respond quickly to both problems and opportunities. Use that strength.

5. Be a Problem Solver—Be a firefighter and crisis manager. When problems arise, deal with them. Move to where the action is. The business is a larger reflection of you; take care of its needs just as you would take care of your personal needs. Tackle any problem, deal with any crisis, and do it personally.

These aspects of the Achieving Route closely reflect the characteristics of the Personal Achiever, thus creating a compatible route that leads to success. The case study of Darwin Dennison at DINE Systems illustrates this compatibility and success.

Darwin Dennison of DINE Systems

Dennison founded DINE Systems while continuing to work as a professor in the Department of Health Behavioral Sciences at the State University of New York at Buffalo. The development and strategic planning work in which he is most involved at DINE occurs during breaks in the academic calendar—in the summer, the spring, and between semesters. The company is a software publishing firm specializing in nutrient analysis and diet improvement. Products are marketed to both health professionals and direct consumers. The company receives income from research grants obtained from both the federal government and the state. Early on it operated in a technology development center, or incubator, subsequently moving to a commercial facility.

DINE has grown at a rate of approximately two employees per year to its current size of 20. Annual revenues now approximate $1 million, and the company is profitable. There have been some ups and downs, but the research grants provide a good buffer against recession. The company is moving increasingly into consumer markets, and there are plans for continued expansion; R&D remains important, but less so than in the past. Overall this is a major success story, although DINE is still small, as are its competitors.

Dennison has been president of the company from its beginning. His psychological profile indicates average strengths as a Real Manager entrepreneur, and even more as an Expert Idea Generator entrepreneur, but it is the energy he puts into his company and his work (his Personal Achiever qualities) that comes through as most characteristic. He is highly motivated to achieve on his own, to set goals and plan for future company growth, and to compare his performance against various indexes of success along the way. To his way of thinking, what others in positions of power do, and chance events, have very little to do with his outcomes. What really matters is what he does, and that incites him to do the best he possibly can. He has a large amount of nervous energy and maintains a rather high level of tension, but he likes to be challenged and would be uncomfortable not being active, if not even somewhat driven. Knowledge is important to him, especially as it relates to his profession and his business. He has a strong personal commitment to both. Work that permits a high degree of individual effort and accomplishment is what really turns him on; group endeavor where decisions are shared is not very attractive.

This strong Personal Achiever pattern is clearly evident in the following profile:

Need to achieve	*Very High*
Desire for feedback	*High*
Desire to plan and set goals	*Very High*
Strong personal initiative	*Not a Factor*
Strong personal commitment to their organization	*High*
Belief that one person can make a difference	*Very High*
Belief that work should be guided by personal goals, not those of others	*Very High*

As is typical of people like this, Dennison throws himself completely into all aspects of his work. He writes books, articles, research proposals, and the software. He is a strong proponent of the free enterprise system and of reward based on individual performance. He has not stopped learning since he obtained his doctorate in health education from West Virginia University a number of years ago; currently he is immersed in managerial accounting. When conflicts emerge within the company, he steps in with a solution. Crises are not allowed to get out of hand. Plans are in place for future growth. Dennison is involved in every aspect of his business including financing (with a Small Business Administration loan) and quality control, which is absolutely crucial. He himself is well informed in a number of technological areas, but consultants provide needed expertise as well. Market planning and development are a particular concern. Sales and marketing are not part of his background and he needs help in this area. Characteristically, Dennison recognizes the need and meets the challenge by hiring those who can help him. Like many people with advanced degrees, he prefers people who are both bright and well educated. DINE has a quality senior management team, consisting of (in addition to himself) Thomas Golaszewski, Dominic Galante, Barry Williams, Roberta Burstein-Markel, and Deborah Weese, all of whom have graduate degrees. He does not mind paying to get what he wants. His goal is not personal wealth, but a successful, competitive business and the reputation that goes with it.

Up to now, it has been possible to run DINE, and to grow it, with a highly personal style. There are not a lot of rules, procedures, standardized systems, and the like. There is outside competition, but the company is at the forefront in technological innovation and with a large number of overweight people as well as hypertensives, diabetics, athletes, and others concerned with improving their diets in the population, the market is there. Accordingly, the company should grow and prosper for some time under the kind of high personal energy system that Dennison finds so compatible.

GETTING STARTED ON
THE ACHIEVING ROUTE

Personal Achievers can start their entrepreneurial career from a variety of places. Of the 100 established entrepreneurs from Western New York State whom I studied, 29 were Personal Achievers. Table 1 shows that about the same number started their firms without partners (24%) as with partners (21%).

Personal Achievers are especially likely to take over a family business (35%). Owners of family businesses should be encouraged by this; if the members in their new generation are Personal Achievers and thus possess the energy and the talent to make these firms grow, they appear to have just as much to offer as the firms' founders. The case of Richard Pohlman of Pohlman Foundry in Chapter 1 illustrates this.

Table 1   HOW PERSONAL ACHIEVERS
BECOME ENTREPRENEURS

Started Firm Without Partners	24%
Started Firm with Partners	21
Purchased Firm	10
Took Over Family Firm	35
Initiated Corporate Venture	10
Was Turnaround Person in Corporate Venture	0
Started Sales or Professional Practice	0
Total	100%

Personal Achievers did not settle for a sales or professional practice—for example, lawyer, accountant, manufacturer's representative. This is understandable; business growth gives Personal Achievers feedback about their actions, but in sales and professional practices, growth is not a primary objective and thus these businesses are not attractive to Personal Achievers.

Nor were Personal Achievers found in corporate turnaround groups, working to improve the operations of either a small business or a subsidiary of a large business. Turnaround specialists often own little or none of the firm, and thereby lack the degree of control over the firm that Personal Achievers want.

Even though Personal Achievers have preferred starting points for becoming entrepreneurs—starting the firm with or without partners and taking over a family business—the starting points that lead to success are varied. And equally varied are the ways that Personal Achievers reach their starting points; some go directly from school to the venture, others go from a nonentrepreneurial job to the venture, or from being unemployed to the venture, or from home to the venture. Several variants exist on each theme.[1]

SUCCESS ON THE ACHIEVING ROUTE

Table 2 shows the success of these 29 Personal Achievers. Some have left their firms to start new ventures or for a nonentrepreneurial career, but 52 percent of them remained with their firms and these firms experienced very substantial growth (expanded sales, increased numbers of employees, and/or greater profits).

Table 2   HOW THE PERSONAL
ACHIEVERS' FIRMS SUCCEEDED

Entrepreneur and Firm Stayed Together	
Firm Has Grown a Lot	52%
Firm Has Grown Some	24
Recession Has Hurt Firm	3
Firm Has Only Survived	0
Entrepreneur and Firm No Longer Together	
Left Firm and Started New Venture	3
Left Firm and Had Nonentrepreneurial Career Subsequently	7
Insufficient Information Available	11
Total	100%

This degree of success is no coincidence. Of the 100 established entrepreneurs, 27 did not score high enough on any pattern to be classified as Personal Achievers, Supersalespeople, Real Managers, or Expert Idea Generators; there was no basis on which to project entrepreneurial success for these people. And by and large, they had little success. None of their firms were in the category, Firm Has Grown a Lot, compared to the 52 percent of the Personal Achievers whose firms were in this category.

Personal Achievers must couple their high energy levels with a firm in which they can put that energy to work in a satisfying way. The catalyst for this process is sufficient knowledge about the specific business and its industry. This knowledge may be very complex, requiring a long period of prior learning, or relatively simple, requiring only minimal preparation. It may be gained primarily before joining the firm, or after.

Learning-on-the-Job as an Entrepreneur

Personal Achievers can learn on the entrepreneurial job using a couple of strategies. First, they may simply hire the know-how (a consultant or a full-time employee) or bring in a partner; then they learn from this person. However, in using this strategy, the Personal Achiever risks ceding a large degree of power to the expert by virtue of the expert's knowledge—power that may be misused. Yet this strategy is employed, often with considerable success, as illustrated in the case in Chapter 1 about Stovroff and Taylor Travel's Jacqueline Taylor, who employed a consultant for several years.

As a second strategy, some businesses can start very small, perhaps as a one-person operation, and grow gradually as the Personal Achiever learns the business. Usually these are relatively simple businesses, requiring less knowledge. And the small size of the business during its early stage reduces the risk of financial loss and the risk of using this strategy. This type of on-the-job learning is illustrated in the case of Harold Hibbard of United Building Services, who started this contract cleaning business as a one-person operation.

Harold Hibbard of United Building Services

United Building Services is in the contract cleaning business. It provides building maintenance and janitorial services to customers throughout Western New York, extending as far east as Rochester. These services include general office cleaning, carpet care, floor care, and specialty work. The company places a strong emphasis on quality and devotes more time to employee training and development than most similar firms. It has four locations and has been particularly effective in contracting for jobs in small towns within its geographical area.

Hibbard started the company before he was 20, doing odd cleaning jobs for commercial and residential clients himself. Gradually work crews were added and the company has come to concentrate entirely on its commercial accounts. Today it has over 300 employees, is approaching $3 million in annual sales volume, and produces a profit, which although not large by some standards, has been maintained consistently over a number of years and is increasing.

Above all Hibbard is a Personal Achiever in the classic tradition. He comes from an entrepreneurial family and has himself owned several other small firms in addition to United Building Services, including a janitorial service in Tampa, Florida, that he ultimately sold and a separate carpet cleaning business, which is currently inactive. In addition to his predominant Personal Achiever pattern, he is also a Supersalesperson, although this factor is somewhat less evident in his work behavior at present.

One source of his high energy is Hibbard's strong desire to achieve through his own efforts. He takes pride in his accomplishments, works extremely hard, and likes to compare evidence of how well he is doing against established standards. The turnover rate among his employees is well below the industry average, for example, and that is a source of satisfaction to him, as well as a major selling point. He feels that what happens to him and his company is not a consequence of external events or luck, but rather a direct result of how well he performs. He has a strong sense of time urgency, a hard-driving orientation, and a certain impatience with situations that temporarily block his achievement strivings. As a consequence, he lives much of the time with a considerable degree of tension and stress. He enjoys learning new things, especially as they relate to his company. The mission of the company—emphasizing quality, reacting to customer needs, maintaining high values, providing honest work, and establishing fair pricing—is his mission as well. He enjoys making the key decisions and serving as a model for others in the firm.

As you might expect, Hibbard is very high on a number of Personal Achiever characteristics.

Need to achieve	*Very High*
Desire for feedback	*Very High*
Desire to plan and set goals	*Not a Factor*
Strong personal initiative	*Not a Factor*
Strong personal commitment to their organization	*Very High*
Belief that one person can make a difference	*Very High*
Belief that work should be guided by personal goals, not those of others	*Very High*

Although he considers himself an operations person, Hibbard has done most of the selling over the history of the company. He also does all the estimating for contract purposes and is involved in every phase of the business. The net result of all this is that even though he is extremely busy and works with an incredible amount of energy, he often becomes a bottleneck and things do not get done simply because he cannot get to them. The company runs not so much according to plan as according to what and when Hibbard is able to devote his energies to things. Yet there are always new projects in some phase of development—setting up to operate boilers in schools and hospitals, looking into buying a new building, establishing a merit pay system, expanding the Rochester operation, selecting people for key jobs; the list is never ending. Yet Hibbard would not have it any other way. The company is his life, and he thoroughly enjoys the rapid pace that it demands of him.

Learning Before Joining the Firm

Jacqueline Taylor of Stovroff and Taylor Travel and Harold Hibbard show how Personal Achievers learn on the job. Personal Achievers more typically learn through some combination of schooling and nonentrepreneurial work prior to entering into the venture.

Sometimes the idea for an entrepreneurial venture arises from the Personal Achiever's schooling or nonentrepreneurial work; sometimes the idea precedes it, and the learning and work experience is specifically crafted to fit the needs of the venture. I believe the latter approach works better, because the Personal Achiever plans more thoroughly. An illustration is John Panarites.

John Panarites of Applied Design Company and Reyco Industries

Applied Design is a Buffalo-area manufacturer of metal and plastic reusable shipping containers that are marketed nationwide. John Panarites bought into the company and managed it from $6 million in sales to almost $14 million in five and a half years. During this period, its profits grew steadily and the number of employees rose to 200. When the company was sold at a substantial profit, Panarites stayed on as president and CEO for a time under contract, and then left. His ownership share when he sold was just under 50 percent, but there was no controlling interest; had he been the primary owner, he probably would not have agreed to the sale.

After considering several positions in which he would have held managerial and/or ownership status, Panarites ended with Reyco Industries in Springfield, Missouri, a supplier of tractor-trailer springs, air suspensions, and brake drums. He and a small group of investors bought the company, and several others to form a composite firm with $70 million in sales and 400 employees. Reyco is the largest component of the composite. It has reduced personnel while doubling sales volume during the time Panarites has been there. The price of materials has been cut and advanced MRPII computerized systems put in place. The company is developing the air ride suspension market, capturing 25 percent so far. The product line is being broadened and more sophisticated equipment introduced. Further expansion through acquisition is anticipated.

Panarites has an undergraduate degree from Syracuse University in industrial engineering and an MBA from Boston College in finance. Early on he spent time with Litton Industries, where he was involved in buying and selling subsidiary companies. In one way or another his career has been a perpetuation of that experience. He stays in manufacturing, he likes to have an ownership position (a substantial one if possible), and he prefers to operate through a business broker in buying into companies.

As might be anticipated, Panarites has a psychological profile that emphasizes both the Real Manager and the Personal Achiever, but a bit more of the latter than the former. These are the activities that characterize his career, and in actualizing his capabilities, he has been quite successful. So have Applied Design and Reyco Industries.

Panarites is a Personal Achiever, above and beyond his managerial capabilities. He enjoys the experience of personal causation and hard work that goes with growing a company. Knowing how well he is doing and comparing company growth against benchmarks is important to him. Planning is somewhat less attractive, but he has come to appreciate it more over time, and to get better at it as well. In the end he believes that what he does makes the biggest difference, and thus planning is worth the effort. He operates under considerable time pressure, with a great deal of drive and tension. Problems do not go away when the normal workday is over. He is a self-starter who prefers to make his own decisions. He often finds himself working with others simply to put together enough capital to make his deals work, but his ideal operating approach is to run things himself. To the extent he can do this, he becomes very committed to his company and to making it a success.

Panarites' personality pattern as a Personal Achiever reveals substantial entrepreneurial strength:

Need to achieve	*Very High*
Desire for feedback	*High*
Desire to plan and set goals	*Not a Factor*
Strong personal initiative	*High*
Strong personal commitment to their organization	*High*
Belief that one person can make a difference	*High*
Belief that work should be guided by personal goals, not those of others	*Very High*

Panarites is a deal maker, building on his Litton experience. Once he is into a company, he puts a tremendous amount of energy into cutting costs, increasing sales, establishing efficiencies, and implementing strategies. Yet he is always on the lookout for new acquisitions and opportunities. This has been the pattern at both Applied Design and Reyco, and in all likelihood it will repeat itself several more times before his career ends. The important point to note, however, is that Panarites is not simply a buy-sell artist. He throws himself into his companies, works on their problems, and adds a great deal of value to them. He often builds a completely new management team in the process. By the time he leaves, the firm is a much stronger organization than when he arrived.

AVOIDING THE TRAPS ALONG THE ACHIEVING ROUTE

Although the Achieving Route is well marked—Be Energetic, Learn, Plan, Be Flexible, and Be a Problem Solver—Personal Achievers may have their energies diverted from this preferred route and end up someplace quite distant: failure.

Here are the traps along the Achieving Route and how to avoid them or escape from them.

The Personal Achiever Lacks the Necessary Knowledge

Personal Achievers may fail to acquire the necessary business knowledge, knowledge that allows them to fully use their talents. As a result, they may completely misdirect their energies.

The antidote: Before entering the venture, determine what knowledge is needed, whether it can be gained before entering the venture, and if so, how to gain it (schooling or a nonentrepreneurial job). If the knowledge can be learned on the entrepreneurial job, determine how to gain it and whether a knowledgeable partner, consultant, or employee should be involved until that knowledge is learned, or whether an academic course would fill the need. Remember how Darwin Dennison, the university professor who runs DINE Systems, learns new subjects as needed and hires key employees who have skills he lacks. But regardless of how much knowledge Personal Achievers have when they join their firms, they rarely have "enough" knowledge; learning must continue. Even with incomplete knowledge, they can still succeed, but a complete lack of knowledge almost always guarantees failure.

The Personal Achiever Does Not Know That He or She Is a Personal Achiever

Personal Achievers may not know their strengths (they may not know they are Personal Achievers) and that the Achieving Route provides the best environment for their capabilities. The younger the Personal Achiever, the more likely this is to occur, because they may lack the experience to know what works or does not work for them.

The antidote: Read this book, or employ a consultant who can assess your capabilities and advise you about the appropriate path to follow. Even

Personal Achievers with considerable experience, and yet an unsuccessful record, can benefit from advice that shows them how to get onto the Achieving Route.

The Personal Achiever Is Prevented from Following the Achieving Route

Three instances can prevent Personal Achievers from following the Achieving Route. First, in corporate venturing or turnaround situations, corporate officers (for whatever strategic reasons) may step in and restrict the unstructured style of Personal Achievers. In my studies, I find that corporate venturing frequently produces rapid turnover among Personal Achievers, because these entrepreneurs are kept from using their talents, kept from being themselves.

Second, much like corporate officers, bankers or venture capitalists may impose an approach on Personal Achievers other than the Achieving Route, thus unwittingly thwarting the venture at an early point. Family members who retain a sizable ownership share may do the same in family businesses.

Third, the Personal Achiever will devote substantial amounts of time to the business, which if family members are not in the business, inevitably restricts family time, thus producing conflict and feelings of rejection. Divorce may be the ultimate result, unless some alternative is found.

Once Personal Achievers enter the Achieving Route, they are rarely diverted from it; it is simply too satisfying to everything they are made of—and too highly reinforced by a capitalistic economic system as well. Thus, in a conflict with corporate officers, bankers, venture capitalists, or family members, the Personal Achiever is unlikely to be the one to give way.

The antidote: Somehow the person who is thwarting the pursuit of the Achieving Route must better understand the Personal Achiever and the Achieving Route and be induced to back away and accept the Personal Achiever's style. Again, reading this book or employing a consultant may be helpful.

The Company Gets Too Big for the Personal Achiever Style

The Achieving Route works well for relatively small organizations. But when firms grow as Personal Achievers want them to grow, they reach a size that demands more than the Personal Achiever can provide. With entrepreneurial success comes a need for structure, hierarchy, and management. Then the Achieving Route is too unstructured, and the Personal Achiever becomes a bottleneck.

This situation may be likened to that of marathon runners who "hit the wall" of fatigue at a point in the race and have to overcome exhaustion to even finish.[2]

At some point as the firm grows, Personal Achievers must realize that they have created a business that they no longer fully understand and are unable to control. In my experience, this phenomenon occurs as an organization grows to have about 30 employees and/or sales of $4 or $5 million. However, problems can begin well before that, especially if the firm is under stress from the outside, such as unusually intense competition or an investigation by government regulators.

Hitting the wall in this manner can mean the end of growth: Personal Achievers may plateau the business and settle for what they can handle using the Achieving Route. Alternatively, they may try to grow the business further, while still using the Achieving Route. That will not work any longer, but the Personal Achiever typically finds this out too late. The result may be bankruptcy, a takeover by creditors, a forced sale; they lose control of the business and are pushed out.

The antidote: Put management and structure into the previously unstructured firm. If the Personal Achiever is also a Real Manager, this transition presents few problems; Personal Achievers merely shift gears, emphasizing a new aspect of their repertoire of talents. This may, however, be impossible, because the Personal Achiever lacks the complex talent required. At this point, to retain control of the firm, a Personal Achiever must adjust: retain strategic control but sacrifice power over day-to-day operations; bring in a managed and structured hierarchy to cope with increased size, including someone to manage the business on a day-to-day basis. With appropriate attention and guidance, Personal Achievers can handle this transition and retain control, but it is often a delicate balancing act.

However, the problems do not end necessarily when firms shift from the Achieving Route to being managed. Growth continues, often phenomenal growth. Yet for a number of reasons, even these very large firms ultimately face the prospect of decline. Just as certain psychological dynamics may limit the use of the Achieving Route, other dynamics can limit the use of a managed hierarchy.[3] In these large firms, there is a risk that strategies will ultimately lead to overexpansion, that goals will extend beyond growth to grandeur, that organizational cultures will take on the character of game playing, and that structure will become excessively fractured.[4] This phenomenon occurs in the world's largest corporations; Personal Achievers must be aware that it can also occur as their firms grow large.

CONCLUSION

When successful, Personal Achievers follow the career path that best fits their personalities, the Achieving Route:

1. They are energetic, throwing themselves into the venture.
2. They learn whatever is necessary to run the business.
3. They plan goals, as well as strategies and timetables to reach them, and they constantly refine these along the way.
4. They are flexible, keeping the venture unstructured and responsive to opportunities and threats.
5. They solve problems, personally dealing with crises and the needs of the organization.

Personal Achievers must avoid the traps of the Achieving Route:

1. They may not have sufficient knowledge to run the organization.
2. They may not understand that they are Personal Achievers who must follow the Achieving Route to be successful.
3. They may be prevented from following the Achieving Route by corporate officers, bankers, or venture capitalists who want to impose structure and hierarchy on the organization.
4. They may have conflicts with the needs of family members who resent the large amount of time and energy they invest in the venture.
5. They may stay on the Achieving Route even when the organization reaches a size that requires more structure.

The case studies in this chapter and in Chapter 1 demonstrate the wide variety of Personal Achievers, their entrepreneurial starting points, and their approaches to gaining the knowledge needed by their firms. To succeed, Personal Achievers must be entrepreneurs, and to succeed as entrepreneurs, they must follow the Achieving Route.

NOTES

1. These starting points and their variants are discussed at length in Karl H. Vesper's book *New Venture Strategies*.
2. W. Gibb Dyer explains this analogy in his book *The Entrepreneurial Experience*.
3. This point is elaborated in an article by Harry Levinson that appeared in *American Psychologist*.
4. In his book *The Icarus Paradox*, Danny Miller describes this process and ties it directly to firms emerging from a Personal Achiever entrepreneur tradition.

CHAPTER 3

The Supersalesperson Entrepreneur

Supersalespeople differ sharply from Personal Achievers. They can be just as successful, but they get there in a very different way, relying on a whole new set of personal characteristics. Unlike the Personal Achiever, this is not a type of person who in the past has been viewed as having the potential to be a successful entrepreneur.[1] This chapter paints a picture of these Supersalespeople entrepreneurs, and then in Chapter 4 I will focus on how Supersalespeople can pursue a career to entrepreneurial success.

WHAT MAKES A SUPERSALESPERSON

The most distinctive thing about Supersalespeople is their approach to selling. They truly cater to the needs of clients and customers, thus placing a strong stress on service. This service emphasis is in contrast to a sales process that is more concerned with managing the customer into a sale through heavy persuasion and pressure tactics.[2] The characteristics of a Supersalesperson entrepreneur all relate in one way or another to this service emphasis.

Supersalespeople may vary among themselves in the mix of these five characteristics, but all possess a majority of them. (Note how different these people are from the hard-driving Personal Achievers.) There are five somewhat overlapping characteristics of the Supersalesperson pattern:

1. Capacity to understand and feel with another (to empathize)
2. Desire to help others
3. Belief that social processes are very important

4. Need to have strong positive relationships with others

5. Belief that a sales force is crucial to carrying out company strategy

Capacity to Understand and Feel with Another

The capacity to understand and feel with another involves many elements. Let's first look at how these elements apply to the individual and then their effect on decision making.

Supersalespeople emphasize human interaction, feelings, and emotions.[3] Often Supersalespeople focus on the past more than the present or future. They are spontaneous, persuasive, empathic, loyal, probing, and introspective; they grasp traditional values and draw out the feelings of others.

They like harmony, need praise occasionally, dislike telling people unpleasant things, and relate well to most other people. They tend to engage in a high degree of conformity and to accommodate themselves to other people.

They are good listeners, very supportive, receptive to suggestions, warm, use persuasion, accept loose control, and prefer oral to written communication. They tend to focus on short-run problems and are action rather than planning oriented. They have little tolerance for ambiguity. They have a talent for building teams, encourage participation at work, and like to hold meetings. They prefer organizations that are well designed, people oriented, collegial.[4]

Because Supersalespeople are well aware of other people and their feelings, they make decisions based on extremely personal conditions, gossip, hearsay, and the like. They personalize each situation by stressing its uniqueness, and how an individual will respond to a decision.

Consequently, in their problem solving, Supersalespeople enjoy pleasing others, dislike dealing with problems that require them to face the unpleasant, are responsive and sympathetic to others' problems, emphasize the human aspects in dealing with managerial concerns, and view problems of inefficiency and ineffectiveness largely in terms of interpersonal and human difficulties.

When avoidance or smoothing over differences is not possible, Supersalespeople are apt to change their positions to ones more acceptable to others. Establishing and maintaining friendly relations can be more important than a concern for achievement, effectiveness, and precise decision making. For example, they may have a difficult time discharging subordinates for inadequate performance.

Thus, if there is any negative about Supersalespeople, it is that they may be too concerned about others, perhaps a bit overly sensitive; they can have difficulty making hard decisions and saying no. They can even be impulsive, sentimental, subjective, and procrastinating; as a result they may unintentionally create conflict. Yet overall the positives outweigh the negatives.

Desire to Help Others

A desire to help others characterizes the helping professions (like medicine and the ministry) particularly, but is inherent in most professional work. Supersalespeople want to assist people with their problems and do for them what they cannot do for themselves. Many sales occupations such as those in the insurance, real estate, and financial products areas have much in common with the professions in this respect, and in fact often are considered semiprofessional in nature.

The desire to help others with their problems may arise entirely out of a strong concern for others, a warm and understanding need to be of service to those who need assistance. It may also on occasion be tinged with a sense of internal satisfaction on the part of Supersalespeople stemming from the recognition that they are strong enough to give help rather than having to receive it.[5]

Belief That Social Processes Are Very Important

A belief that social processes are very important reflects a person's work values. Supersalespeople consider social processes to have a great deal of importance in their lives. They value such things as making a contribution to society, having coworkers who are pleasant and agreeable, being valued as a person and thus having the esteem of others, having the opportunity to meet people and interact with them, and receiving recognition from others for doing a good job. Social interaction and relationships with people are simply more important than many other considerations for supersalespeople.

Need to Have Strong Positive Relationships with Others

Supersalespeople derive satisfaction from good personal relations with others. In fact they may need good relations in order to feel at ease with themselves. Their self-esteem is somewhat dependent on how others regard them. Thus they are concerned about what others think and are sensitive to what people around them feel. Encouraging those with whom they work to participate in decision making and to offer new ideas or a different approach to a problem comes easily to them. When describing a person they find very difficult to work with, they are likely to say—

You may be a very poor coworker, you may be frustrating, inefficient, or lazy. But the coworker role is just one of many, and that doesn't mean that you might not be quite pleasant or worthwhile in other respects.[6]

There is thus a tendency to see the best in others and to feel that doing work efficiently is not the only basis for defining a person's worth.

In leadership roles their concern for others' feelings enables them to obtain group support. If group conflict exists, or if the group's support of a leader should be only lukewarm, Supersalespeople can work around this by being tactful and sensitive to problems before they damage productivity. Where control over those who work for them is very uncertain, however, Supersalespeople may become so concerned with seeking group support that they fail to get the job done. Thus there are situations in which they are not very effective managers.

Belief That a Sales Force Is Crucial to Carrying Out Company Strategy

Supersalespeople consider the sales force to be an important means of implementing company strategies. Relative to other available approaches such as advertising, delivery, discounts, new product development, packaging, price, quality, reciprocity, reputation, services, and variety, the sales force stands very high in their minds. It may not always be the single most dominant approach, but if not, it is unlikely to lag far behind.

WHAT SUPERSALESPEOPLE LOOK LIKE

Unlike Personal Achievers, Supersalespeople do not have to become entrepreneurs to fully utilize their talents and achieve real satisfaction. Many remain employed by corporations throughout their careers. Opportunities and the pressure of circumstances can play a major role here. The key point, however, is that Supersalespeople can start ventures and have successful careers as entrepreneurs.

To illustrate this fact I present two case studies dealing with the characteristics of Supersalespeople and how they achieved success. Richard Page is founder of Woodstream Nurseries. Joseph Doro heads Doro's Dry Cleaning.

Richard Page of Woodstream Nurseries

Woodstream Nurseries was started by two partners who went to college together. After about 10 years Richard Page bought out his partner and the latter left the business. Since that time the company has grown a great deal. The largest business sector is in contract landscaping, which includes design and construction. The company also does a good business in wholesaling to other nurseries and to institutions. Maintenance services such as snowplowing are provided, and the company owns two retail outlets that are contributing an increasing share to total sales. The firm's market area extends throughout Western New York, including Buffalo and Rochester.

The number of employees varies with the season. It grows to 85 during the summer months; during the winter offseason it is about 25. Sales are now up to well over $2 million a year. The company has remained profitable almost every year, although as is typical where retail sales are an important component, margins are not large.

In recent years Page has made an effort to cut back on his activities, due to some health problems, but he continues as president and also makes sales to customers, particularly in the contract landscaping area. His forte is as a Supersalesperson. There is some strength as well in Expert Idea Generation, which is reflected primarily in the design work he does in connection with making landscaping sales and in planning for the business. Although Page may well have been a Personal Achiever at one time and still shows some strong vestiges of that pattern, this is not a major characteristic at present.

What is most pronounced is the desire to interact with other people, both inside and outside the business. He is spontaneous, persuasive, empathic, and loyal; grasps the values of others; and draws out other people's feelings. Telling people unpleasant things does not come easily to him. He likes to create a friendly, agreeable atmosphere, which usually means seeing the best in other people. Being personally liked and valued by others is important. He prefers a certain loose, informal type of control that seems conducive to building team spirit and trust. Helping others to deal with their problems is important to him. One of his company's most important strategies is said to be the effective use of a good sales force. Giving these people, and other employees as well, full credit for what they accomplish is simply part of his nature.

On the five components of the Supersalesperson pattern Page scores very high or high on all.

Capacity to understand and feel with another	*Very High*
Desire to help others	*High*

Belief that social processes are very important   *High*
Need to have strong positive relationships with others   *Very High*
Belief that a sales force is crucial to carrying
  out company strategy   *Very High*

Page has always been a major factor in the company's sales growth. He is out of the office much of the time talking to customers and potential customers. This is when he is in his element, and he does very well at it. Even when he does not seem to be selling, or perhaps even to realize it, he is selling. He is very active in various trade associations, in the Buffalo Executives Association, and in other business or business-related groups. This networking brings in a lot of work for the company.

A by-product of this style, however, is that the company needs people to manage the business, handle financial affairs, and provide expert advice. It is to Page's credit that he recognized this need early on and did something to take care of it. He has put together a strong management team that has stayed with him. He meets with them as a group often and the discussion is very much two-way. He is in the process of releasing part of his ownership to this group. There is a lot of delegation. This extends to his accounting and legal advisors, who have remained the same over a number of years. The structure that has emerged is one where Page himself does the outside networking, the planning, and a not inconsiderable amount of the selling, while a team of managers and experts actually run the business on a day-to-day basis.

Joseph Doro of Doro's Dry Cleaning Company

Joe Doro is the third generation of his family to head the company; he has only recently taken over from his father. The business started as a tailor shop with garment cleaning as a sideline. Gradually the work shifted so that dry cleaning of garments became the dominant activity. That business remains today, serving a local clientele, which includes some commercial work with hotels in the area. It accounts for roughly 10 percent of the company's income.

The major part of the business, however, is a Coit franchise. Coit, a San Francisco–based operation with some 50 franchises around the country, is the world's largest drapery, carpet, upholstery, and area rug cleaning organization. The concept is to deliver to the marketplace complete home cleaning services. This is done primarily using specially equipped trucks that are able to do much of the cleaning on site. The Coit Drapery and Carpet Cleaners franchise operates as a subsidiary of Doro's Dry Cleaning. It struggled for a number of years and did not represent a significant proportion of the business until Joe Doro took it over. Since then it has grown steadily. At present it serves a sizable area around Buffalo, extending east to beyond Rochester.

Doro's Dry Cleaning Company as a whole employs some 50 people and now exceeds the $2 million mark in annual sales. It is the nature of the business that it is very labor intensive, requiring different people to carry out the different processes. The local dry cleaning activity is stable, but the Coit activity has been growing steadily, showing relatively little effect from recession. There is considerable potential for further growth since the franchise territory extends clear across the state to Albany.

Joe Doro's psychological profile indicates that he is primarily a Supersalesperson with significant secondary strength in the managerial area. What he is not is the Personal Achiever that has come to represent the stereotype of the classic entrepreneur. The managerial pattern is such that he should be able to operate as his own general manager for the business rather than bringing in someone for that purpose, as is often required when Supersalespeople become entrepreneurs. It is also true, however, that Real Managers (as will be discussed in Chapter 5) often turn out to be effective salespeople whenever they are able to manage the customer into a purchase.

Thus, Joe Doro appears to have the characteristics of a successful salesperson on two counts—a hard-sell aspect and the soft-sell, empathic aspect, which is the more dominant in his case. In this latter regard his sincere desire to help others is a major factor. He really wants to help others and make life easier for them. He cares about people and is concerned for their feelings. At times he is troubled that he does not listen well enough to what others are saying, that he is too overpowering. This may be a natural consequence when hard and soft-sell patterns are combined in the same person. In any event he likes to meet people, enjoys working in a pleasant and agreeable social context, wants to contribute to society by helping people, and desires the esteem of others. He views a good sales force as important to the success of the business. One way or another he is capable of motivating people, both employees and customers. Selling comes naturally to him.

Based on the tests Doro's pattern looks as follows:

Capacity to understand and feel with another	*High*
Desire to help others	*Very High*
Belief that social processes are very important	*High*
Need to have strong positive relationships with others	*Not a Factor*
Belief that a sales force is crucial to carrying out company strategy	*Very High*

Joe Doro started out to be a teacher. He obtained an undergraduate degree in botany and a master's in education from Cornell University, and his first job afterward was teaching agriculture in the public schools of a small New York town. Unfortunately the financial prospects were not good and he ultimately undertook the resurrection of the Coit franchise, starting as a route salesperson. As we have seen, this objective has been well accomplished. He sells himself, he teaches others how to sell, and he really grows the business. He motivates others by working with them as a team, like a group of students. What has happened to the business is a testimonial to the effectiveness of this approach.

CONCLUSION

The characteristics of the Supersalesperson are often overlapping and for that reason these people appear quite similar, irrespective of the specific characteristics. This is more true of this entrepreneurial pattern than of any of the others. All of the five characteristics that help define a Supersalesperson are social in nature, involving other people:

1. Capacity to understand and feel with another
2. Desire to help others
3. Belief that social processes are very important
4. Need to have strong positive relationships with others
5. Belief that a sales force is crucial to carrying out company strategy

Although usually only a majority of these components are present in a given individual, the full array can occur. The tie to selling, and to the Selling Route discussed in the next chapter, is close and compelling.

Supersalespeople relate to others very well, primarily because they understand how these people feel. They are interested in others' problems and try hard to be a friend. Acceptance by others is important; situations that involve conflict and unpleasantness are avoided. Even people seen as difficult to work with are viewed as having positive characteristics in other respects. Working with others in a group context is attractive. Being liked and recognized for doing a good job are key motives. Also meeting people and contributing something to society are important. Helping others deal with their problems is a source of great satisfaction. To others Supersalespeople seem sincerely interested in them. It is hard not to like such people, and even harder not to buy the products or services offered; someone who is that concerned about others deserves something in return. Not surprisingly, a competitive strategy that emphasizes a strong sales force is very attractive to Supersalespeople.

NOTES

1. The importance of marketing and sales processes in entrepreneurship has long been recognized, going back to an early book by Norman R. Smith titled *The Entrepreneur and His Firm: The Relationship Between Type of Man and Type of Company*. However, the idea of a separate sales type of entrepreneur is new.
2. A similar distinction within selling is made by Guy Oakes in his small volume *The Soul of the Salesman*.
3. This is what John W. Slocum and Don Hellriegel stress in their article in *Business Horizons*, as they describe what they call the "feeling" style.
4. This presentation draws on the description of the "behavioral" style contained in *Managing with Style* by Alan J. Rowe and Richard O. Mason. In our analyses we find that these two—what are called the feeling and behavioral styles—are really the same thing.
5. This latter type of helping motivation type is described in detail by David C. McClelland in *Power: The Inner Experience*.
6. This description is taken from *New Approaches to Effective Leadership* by Fred E. Fiedler and Joseph E. Garcia.

CHAPTER 4

How Supersalespeople Succeed or Fail

To succeed Supersalespeople need to sell. This is what comes naturally to them, this is what they do well, and this is how their businesses grow. Their motto should be "Follow the Selling Route to success" (but be sure to find a way to cover for the other necessary business functions too). Chapter 3 provided a picture of what Supersalespeople are like; now I will show how their career should unfold to take the Selling Route and how to avoid the traps that litter the way.

THE SELLING ROUTE

The Selling Route involves three critical aspects:

1. Learning how to sell and learning about the product or service being sold
2. Sticking to selling
3. Providing for backup to handle the other aspects of the business

Supersalespeople typically find sales and marketing at an early age. They are often career salespeople. Sales seems to be in their blood, and indeed many have parents who are in sales also. Even if they do not start out in selling positions, Supersalespeople seem to gravitate in that direction over time.

Because selling is not easily learned in school, Supersalespeople are likely to have fewer years of education and more years of business experience than

Personal Achievers, Real Managers, and Expert Idea Generators. They learn on the job rather than from formal education. And even in their education they tend to concentrate on courses in marketing and communications that relate to the selling process.

Knowledge of the product and/or service being sold is important. Supersalespeople must know the business, but beyond that a person who is to be the premier salesperson should be quite familiar with what is being sold. For Supersalespeople, this product or service familiarity typically is obtained on the job, selling. Usually they start in a junior sales position with another company. In the case of family businesses, people often work their way up through sales and marketing positions within the firm; however, it is not atypical to start a venture directly out of school, selling it into growth from a very small beginning.

A major problem is that when the venture is small Supersalespeople are likely to be continually pulled back into administration and operations simply because there is no one else available. This is less troublesome if the firm is limited to wholesaling or retailing because there is less by way of operations to be drawn into, but it exists even there. To the extent Supersalespeople are not selling, their talent is wasted, they are not following the appropriate route, and the business suffers. They may very well compound this consequence by being overly softhearted, with the result that receivables are not collected, discipline is lax, and the business is not well managed.

The message is clear—stick to selling. This, however, means that you have to provide for backup to handle what you are not doing. This is as much a part of the Selling Route as is selling itself. One approach is to take on a partner or partners; unlike Personal Achievers, Supersalespeople do not mind partners, in fact they rather enjoy them. Such a partner should complement the salesperson by having expertise in finance, the technology of manufacture, purchasing, and the like. An alternative is to take on a general manager or to establish a management team. Ventures where the entrepreneur is following the Selling Route need this backup person or team at a very early point in their development—much earlier than when the Personal Achiever route is involved. If there is no provision for backup, either the entrepreneur is constantly drawn back into the business or the company cannot effectively fill the orders that are generated. The problem becomes less acute if the Supersalesperson is also a Real Manager, a particularly happy circumstance that can totally obviate the need for backup. However, this situation is unlikely to occur often.

Developing a cohesive team to handle backup activities is particularly attractive to many Supersalespeople. They enjoy the social interaction, and they have no special need to feel that they alone are responsible for successful outcomes. For many, working with and developing teams seems to come quite naturally; Supersalespeople are by nature participative, sharing people.[1]

As is often true, Joseph Almeida in the case example that follows is a Supersalesperson who is not a Real Manager. When Almeida felt compelled to be a manager, he and the company stalled completely. At that point Almeida had lost his way and entered on the wrong route. Later he recovered by returning to selling; now a partner provides a good, compatible backup—a general manager in many respects—and there is team building in the picture as well.

Joseph Almeida of Century 21 Almeida Real Estate

Almeida Real Estate was originally formed as a sole proprietorship in Hamburg, New York. It is engaged in residential and commercial marketing, relocation, mortgages, and new home sales. Roughly 80 percent of its business is residential. After five years in business one of the first salespeople hired was taken in as a partner. Also at an early point the firm became part of the Century 21 system, primarily because of the training and relocation advantages this arrangement offered.

The company has grown steadily since its beginning and in recent years quite rapidly. It now employs 60 people in three offices. A major source of this expansion has been the purchase of vacation homes in the ski area south of Buffalo by Canadians. There also has been an increase in work with relocating families, in handling new construction, and in providing more sophisticated financing options for the purchase of real estate.

Joe Almeida is the founder and president of the firm. Although having some strength in the area of Expert Idea Generation, his most pronounced characteristic is as a Supersalesperson. There is little evidence of being either a Personal Achiever or a Real Manager. In fact, Almeida is a rather laid-back Type B, not a Type A person. He is strongly drawn to social interaction, is a good listener, shows warmth toward others, and uses persuasion to get things done. He is the kind of person who accommodates himself to others and tries to avoid disagreements. Helping others is something he likes to do, and that is what he is doing when he finds the right house for a family or sells a house for someone. Having an opportunity to meet people, being valued by others, contributing to society, and working with people who are pleasant and agreeable are the kinds of things most important to him. He views an effective sales force as one of the keys to his firm's success.

This picture plays out in his characteristics:

Capacity to understand and feel with another	*Very High*
Desire to help others	*High*
Belief that social processes are very important	*Very High*
Need to have strong positive relationships with others	*Not a Factor*
Belief that a sales force is crucial to carrying out company strategy	*High*

Consistent with all this, Almeida has indeed been in sales most of his life. His college major was marketing, and he was in real estate with several other firms before going on his own. The division of labor with his partner is that he handles the recruiting, training, and motivating of sales personnel, while also doing considerable selling himself, and the partner who has an MBA runs the office and handles the financial end. This arrangement works well. It is also typical that Almeida has started to use groups to share ideas and build trust within the company.

It should come as no surprise that Almeida is an outstanding real estate salesperson, having won a variety of awards for sales volume. At one point he became heavily involved in managing, because he felt that was what a president should do, and largely gave up selling. In this period the company stopped growing, and he even considered selling out because he did not find the work enjoyable. It was only when he went back to selling, and turned more of the managing over to others, that he began to enjoy his work again. At the same time business picked up and the company began to grow as well. Market share jumped to over 12 percent from what had been less than half of that, in spite of the fact that the competition consists of well over 400 agencies and companies.

Consistent with his sense of community responsibility, Almeida is active in the Jaycees, in the Chamber of Commerce, and in various economic development activities. It is true that as the community grows, Almeida Real Estate grows too, but that is largely a side benefit of a desire to provide help to others. That is the way things work for these Supersalespeople. They want to be with people, and meet new people, and help them, and somehow in the process a sale occurs.

GETTING STARTED ON THE SELLING ROUTE

As with Personal Achievers, Supersalespeople start their ventures in a variety of ways, as shown in Table 3 for the 27 established entrepreneurs from Western New York whom I studied and who qualified as Supersalespeople.

Supersalespeople do start firms, as often with partners as without. I find also that they are more likely than Personal Achievers to accept partners later and less likely to reject partners early on. The whole getting rid of partners process that characterizes Personal Achievers does not seem to be particularly prevalent among Supersalespeople. Even when a partner leaves the firm, another may well come on the scene shortly.

Supersalespeople purchase firms (11 percent) and take over a family business (22 percent) at about the same rate as the 27 entrepreneurs who failed to meet the requirements for any of the four strong entrepreneurial patterns. In this latter respect Supersalespeople differ from Personal Achievers, who tend to be found more frequently in the family firms. Also, Supersalespeople tend not to start corporate ventures, or no-growth sales or professional practices.

SUCCESS ON THE SELLING ROUTE

Table 4 shows that Supersalespeople certainly can grow a very successful venture.

The big successes are not quite as evident in Table 4 as they were in Table 2 for Personal Achievers (only 30 percent of Supersalespeople had firms in the Firm Has Grown a Lot category, as opposed to 52 percent in

Table 3   HOW SUPERSALESPEOPLE BECOME ENTREPRENEURS

Started Firm Without Partners	26%
Started Firm with Partners	26
Purchased Firm	11
Took Over Family Firm	22
Initiated Corporate Venture	0
Was Turnaround Person in Corporate Venture	11
Started Sales or Professional Practice 4	
Total	100%

Table 4   HOW THE SUPERSALESPEOPLE'S
FIRMS SUCCEEDED

Entrepreneur and Firm Stayed Together	
Firm Has Grown a Lot	30%
Firm Has Grown Some	33
Recession Has Hurt Firm	15
Firm Has Only Survived	0
Entrepreneur and Firm No Longer Together	
Left Firm and Started New Venture	7
Left Firm and Had Nonentrepreneurial Career Subsequently	4
Insufficient Information Available	11
Total	100%

Table 2). This may be partially due to Supersalespeople not being as recession resistant. But even though they tend to experience slower growth, none of the firms were in the "Firm Has Only Survived" category. In contrast among the 27 entrepreneurs who lack a strong pattern of any kind, 30 percent of their firms were in this "no growth" category. And finally, if a Supersalesperson does leave the firm for some reason, the likelihood is that he or she will subsequently start a new venture, not shift to a career outside entrepreneurship.

All this is good news for Supersalespeople, at least as long as they hold to the Selling Route. Yet they may experience some vulnerability. Recession clearly can hurt. Other factors can divert a person from the Selling Route, at least temporarily. We see some hint of these problems in the previous case of Joe Almeida. To understand them more clearly we need to look at additional instances: Thomas Hughes of Rainbow Fashions and Anthony Mancuso of Elrae Industries.

Thomas Hughes of Rainbow Fashions at Orchard Park

The firm was originally formed by Tom Hughes, his wife Sheila, and another couple. However, before long the other couple bowed out. Rainbow Fashions provides specialized adaptive and nonadaptive clothing to the elderly, the developmentally disabled and the handicapped, as well as on occasion to the staff of the nursing homes and institutions where it sells its products. Sheila Hughes, an RN, is in fact the primary owner, which entitles the firm to consideration as a minority business.

The company is essentially a "store on wheels," in contrast to most of the competition, which operates on a mail order basis.

In less than 10 years of existence, Rainbow Fashions has grown to 14 employees, most of whom are part time, and almost $300,000 a year in sales. The business is profitable. Considering that the original intent was to provide the Hughes with a part-time activity and a small income, this record is impressive. Tom Hughes developed multiple sclerosis (MS) prior to the founding of the business and has been forced to limit his activities. On the other hand his illness gives him a special understanding of the customer group he serves. An emphasis on quality products and service has contributed to the firm's competitive advantage.

Because of his illness Tom Hughes has had to limit the kinds of things he does, and in particular he has not been able to do the amount of on-site selling he would like. His responsibilities as chief operating officer are to (1) develop and maintain a business plan that ensures continued market penetration and financial growth; (2) oversee and direct the timely augmentation of the business plan; (3) maintain financial integrity; (4) establish and monitor procedures for the efficient operation of a business office, such as telemarketing, purchasing, accounts payable, accounts receivable, and employee relations; and (5) assist in the marketing direction of Rainbow Fashions, its sales staff, and its products. The balance among these has shifted at various times dependent on the state of his health. Roughly 10–15 percent of company sales are telephone catalog sales made directly from the home office.

Tom Hughes has an entrepreneurial profile that is all Supersalesperson. The other scores are average or somewhat below average and would seem to have little to do with the success of the business. Consistent with this pattern, he enjoys making other people happy, is responsive and sympathetic to people's problems, tends to emphasize the human aspects of situations, enjoys the esteem of others and being valued as a person, and likes recognition for performing well. He is very sensitive to the feelings of others and is a good listener. Avoidance of conflict is important, primarily because anything that would hurt others is unpleasant for him. He views service to people as the major force behind what he does. In the process of pursuing this goal he generates so much goodwill that people give him the esteem and recognition that he enjoys; they also give him sales. Not surprisingly, he considers the sales force an essential factor in the business. His personal identity is closely intertwined with selling, as was his father's before him.

Hughes in fact is highest in his ability to understand and feel with others, but there are additional Supersalesperson strengths as well:

Capacity to understand and feel with another	*Very High*
Desire to help others	*Not a Factor*
Belief that social processes are very important	*High*
Need to have strong positive relationships with others	*Not a Factor*
Belief that a sales force is crucial to carrying out company strategy	*Very High*

Consistent with this pattern, Hughes graduated from the University of New Haven with a degree in marketing. He has always worked in sales or marketing. His longest stint by far was with Bethlehem Steel Corporation, where he was recognized as a major contributor to corporate profitability.

At Rainbow Fashions, Sheila Hughes has carried the primary load insofar as on-site visits are concerned, although with some improvement in his health Tom Hughes has been able to do more of this. This is what he loves to do, even to the extent of making cold calls. With changes in the firm's source of accounting input and increased staffing in the office, he has been able to devote more time to what he likes to do—direct selling, selling over the telephone, training sales personnel, and developing the marketing effort as a whole. As a consequence the business has prospered, and he no longer talks of selling out. He is having fun.

Anthony Mancuso of Elrae Industries

Elrae Industries is a diversified producer of stamped and roll-formed components for the automotive, bicycle, computer, furniture, appliance, and electronics industries as well as for the military. Its products are sold primarily to original equipment manufacturers. The company offers a combination of metalworking and service capabilities including online computerized ordering, statistical process control of operations, just-in-time delivery, welding, and assembly. The workforce is highly skilled, has the capacity to create innovative solutions to customer problems, and manufactures quality products for a wide range of customers.

A little history is required to understand how Elrae got to its present position. When Mancuso joined the company as general manager, it was externally owned and almost exclusively a supplier to the bicycle industry. However, as fenders disappeared and production moved off-shore, this market shrank precipitously. The need for new markets was met by mounting a major sales effort aimed at the automotive industry. Sales of trim parts, particularly to General Motors, increased sharply. Also, Mancuso and four minority stockholders bought the company in a leveraged buyout. After a period of renewed success in the automotive industry, that market also began to disappear with the shift from metal to plastic trim parts. Again a sales effort was mounted, this time aimed at selling a diverse array of products to a number of customers so that the company would not be vulnerable to the loss of a single product or customer. Again the strategy of selling into a new market paid off.

The company has had its ups and downs and has even had a few unprofitable years. Annual sales have on occasion risen well over the $5 million mark. They dropped off somewhat due to the recession, but the company now seems headed for a $6 million year. The number of employees currently is 40. As noted, Mancuso's approach to adversity has consistently involved an emphasis on marketing and developing a new customer base. On the surface this appears unusual because he is an engineer with a general business MBA from the State University of New York at Buffalo and has been employed primarily in operations and general management positions, not sales and marketing.

A look at the psychological profile provides an answer. Two factors are elevated. Consistent with his career pattern Mancuso is an entrepreneur who is also a Real Manager, but even more significant, he possesses the pattern of a Supersalesperson. He likes people, he cares about their needs, and he wants to help them. He has the temperament of a salesperson. There is a strong tendency to see the best in people, even when he knows they are not doing a good job. As a result he appears sensitive, even softhearted. Yet this very quality makes people want to buy what he has to sell. He tends to play up the contributions of others and to play down his own accomplishments. He has a good grasp of markets because he gets to know and understand the people who frequent them.

Mancuso's test patterns reflect this:

Capacity to understand and feel with another	*Very High*
Desire to help others	*Very High*
Belief that social processes are very important	*Not a Factor*
Need to have strong positive relationships with others	*Very High*
Belief that a sales force is crucial to carrying out company strategy	*Not a Factor*

Given these characteristics, Mancuso's almost automatic resort to sales solutions when the going gets difficult is not surprising. It is also not surprising that these marketing efforts tend to succeed. He often involves himself directly in sales situations. Initial contacts with customers are made via telemarketing and manufacturer's representatives, but after that Mancuso as president, along with other members of top management, may arrive on the scene. He tries to call on existing customers as often as he can, and he believes in getting employees out to see them to learn about their needs. He frequently attends trade shows.

This people orientation pervades Mancuso's internal management style as well. The company utilizes work teams and employee involvement techniques extensively, often in conjunction with its quality improvement programs. There is a great deal of concern for the individual employee, to the point where people who are not performing may be retained longer than they would be in other companies. It is hard to take the step of actually letting a person go. Yet this same sensitivity to others leads people to view Elrae as a very good place to work.

Tom Hughes has not been able to sell as much as he would have liked because of his health. The company has survived and prospered, but much of this has been because of his wife's efforts. As his health has improved, the opportunity to sell has increased as well, and Rainbow Fashions is now expanding more rapidly. Anthony Mancuso of Elrae has been caught in a firm that is not consistently large enough to manage, but still on occasion needs his managerial talents. Thus he shifts in and out of the Selling Route. This is working, but it may be that a more consistent dedication to selling would pay off even more in a firm of this size.

What we see is that Supersalespeople can be diverted from the Selling Route by a number of factors; it is not easy to stay focused, and as in the case of Tom Hughes it may even be beyond the Supersalesperson's control. This is what makes Supersalespeople more vulnerable than Personal Achievers. Their talents are more narrowly focused—on sales—and they must keep their eye on the customer bull's-eye.

AVOIDING THE TRAPS ALONG THE SELLING ROUTE

The case examples about Supersalespeople illustrate some of the traps along the Selling Route. Let's now focus on these and other traps and discuss some of the antidotes you may apply to avoid them.

The Supersalesperson Lacks the Necessary Knowledge

To follow the Selling Route you must know your products and services. The trap: You start a venture too soon, before having learned enough, and fail as a result. This is a special problem for Supersalespeople who are just coming out of school. They may know less than they think about the practical realities of selling a particular product.

The antidote: Develop a strategy for learning and be patient. Where can you go to study or work and obtain the best possible information regarding what you are going to sell and how to sell it? The real estate sales experience that Joe Almeida had before starting his own company is a good example of a successful learning strategy.

Also, remember that on the Selling Route, you must have backup in other areas of the business such as finance and operations. Unless you are a Real Manager in addition to a Supersalesperson, learning every aspect of the business is not necessary. It can even divert you from the Selling Route.

The Supersalesperson Does Not Fully Recognize His or Her Talents

In my experience Supersalespeople are more likely to know what they are than Personal Achievers. Yet this is not always the case. In some instances a person fails to recognize a potential for success on the Selling Route and therefore does not follow it.

The antidote: Reading this book should provide the needed understanding. However, it will not necessarily help a Supersalesperson decide whether to follow a sales career working for others or as an entrepreneur. That decision should take into account other strengths and weaknesses, as well as the opportunities available and the pressures operating at the time. Many people are able to make that evaluation for themselves. But sometimes the decision is complex. At such times, consider using a consultant who can assess your capabilities and the business aspects of the situation.

The Supersalesperson Is Forced Off the Selling Route

In many respects this trap operates for Supersalespeople much as it does for Personal Achievers. Corporate officers (with corporate ventures), bankers, venture capitalists, family members, and others may simply push you off the selling road, demanding that you focus on aspects of the business other than selling. Supersalespeople are particularly vulnerable to this problem because they want others to like them, so they attempt to avoid conflict by going along with pressures from others.

One type of pressure that Personal Achievers often face, however, is much less of a problem for Supersalespeople: pressure from family members outside the firm. If one enjoys social relationships, family interaction is just as attractive as customer interaction. Accordingly, battles over family time are much less likely for Supersalespeople.

The antidote to being diverted from the Selling Route: You must be constantly aware of your vulnerability to pressures from others. If you find yourself not getting much pleasure out of what you are doing, then look to see if you are still on the Selling Route. It may be difficult to get back on, but as people like Joe Almeida and Tony Mancuso demonstrate it can be done. Here too, reading (or rereading) this book and employing a knowledgeable consultant can help.

Traps That Appear as the Firm Grows Larger

There is a limit to the growth a Supersalesperson can generate alone. Pinpointing exactly when this point occurs in the growth of a firm is difficult. In terms of dollar volume of sales it can extend over a wide range, with the specific point depending on the size and time of each sale. Many separate small sales may get a person to the personal limit quite rapidly, and at a dollar amount well below $1 million a year. Large sales are likely to take more time, but when the limit is reached they may yield many millions of dollars. Furthermore, some large sales in certain markets do not take a great deal of time. Overall, selling big ticket items provides an advantage when pursuing the Selling Route.

Reaching the sales limit is akin to "hitting the wall" that Personal Achievers experience. Yet there are differences too. When you follow the Selling Route, you must have managers on board at an early point. Thus when the firm gets to a size where the Supersalesperson cannot do all the selling, there is already a structure in place. If that were not true, the firm would never have gotten this far.

The antidote: When Supersalespeople reach their personal limit, they need to shift over to handling a set of key accounts, while developing a sales force or using manufacturer's representatives to add new business and provide for continued growth. In my experience, one of the best approaches is to create sales teams in which the Supersalesperson participates as a team member.

You may, however, find it hard to give these new people breathing room. They do not seem to work as hard and as long and with as much dedication as you do. Turnover often becomes excessive. There can be a glitch at this point, and it may take a while before the Supersalesperson makes the necessary transition. If he or she does not, the firm plateaus at what the Supersalesperson can sell. This in turn may cause you to become disillusioned, to withdraw from selling, or even to withdraw from the business as a whole. Either way the Supersalesperson–Selling Route fit is severed, and the firm is likely to go into a tailspin. Reaching the limit of one's own personal sales ability can be a very difficult time for both the individual and the company.

Assuming, however, that a company gets over this glitch, develops a full-fledged sales force and grows and grows—Can a bountiful future last forever using the Selling Route? Not necessarily. Decline may occur because the company becomes decoupled from the demands of its markets and begins to drift. Supersalespeople are no longer challenged, they lose interest, and they come to believe the system will continue to work well even without their efforts. Bland proliferation of products comes to replace brilliant marketing strategies. Market share is no longer the goal, only quarterly numbers. The organizational culture becomes insipid and overly political. Running all aspects of the organization falls entirely to the backup administrators and becomes oppressively bureaucratic.[2] The clear message: Supersalespeople can never become complacent and get separated from selling.

CONCLUSION

Supersalesperson entrepreneurs succeed by following the Selling Route with great persistence and arranging for other people to cover the business functions extending beyond selling and marketing.

Supersalespeople need to avoid a number of traps that lie along the Selling Route:

1. They may have insufficient knowledge of the products and services they sell.
2. They may not fully recognize the Supersalesperson within them.
3. They may be forced out of the Selling Route by other people or by circumstances; by their nature, they are particularly susceptible to this trap.
4. They may fail to traverse the growing pains that appear when the Supersalesperson reaches a personal sales limit.

Although Supersalespeople do not necessarily become entrepreneurs, they have the potential for it. Such people can be very successful, if they structure their ventures to provide for the conduct of administrative and operational activities and free themselves to follow the Selling Route. There certainly are other types of salespeople, and I will consider one of these in the next chapter, but there appears to be something about the Supersalesperson that yields a particularly strong potential for creating successful ventures. Why? Because these individuals relate to a broad range of other people in ways that are especially likely to elicit sales. And they establish continuing relationships, which can mean continuing sales.

NOTES

1. A number of sources provide information on team efforts of this kind. The book *Team Entrepreneurship* by Alex Stewart deals specifically with an entrepreneurial context. *The Wisdom of Teams* by Jon R. Katzenbach and Douglas K. Smith provides a wider view of the subject in organizations.
2. This is the picture that Danny Miller paints in *The Icarus Paradox* for large declining firms born of a Supersalesperson tradition.

CHAPTER 5

The Real Manager Entrepreneur

Entrepreneurs carry the same titles as top level corporate managers—president, chief executive officer (CEO), chairman of the board. Thus, we tend to think of entrepreneurs and corporate managers as being the same. But in their personality makeup they typically are not the same.[1] Top corporate executives are unlikely to show the Personal Achiever, Supersalesperson, or Expert Idea Generator patterns. And only some successful entrepreneurs are likely to show the Real Manager pattern. In short, if you are a corporate manager, you have only a limited chance of having entrepreneurial potential. If you are an established entrepreneur, you have only a limited chance of possessing the potential to be a successful corporate manager. This "limited chance" is the ground occupied by Real Manager entrepreneurs.

Real Managers enter into the process of achieving entrepreneurial success in a very special way. Before discussing the characteristics of Real Managers and providing some case examples of this pattern, I must explain how Real Managers fit into the entrepreneurial success puzzle.

Real Managers and Other Entrepreneurial Patterns

Managing, in the sense of corporate management, is not something that is important when ventures are very small, with few employees. To use managerial talent requires having enough people to manage, and an organization with several levels in the management hierarchy as well. We have seen how Personal Achievers and Supersalespeople use the Achieving and Selling Routes to grow ventures from scratch, but managing does not seem to work this way; it is a process for large ventures, not small ones.

When we look closely at the Real Managers among established entrepreneurs, especially those who start businesses, we find that most have at least one other strong entrepreneurial pattern above and beyond being a Real Manager. Most entrepreneurs grow their firms in the early years based on talents other than those of the Real Manager. As the company becomes big enough, the Real Manager pattern kicks in, if it is present. If a small firm is headed by a person with only the Real Manager pattern, a compatible partner who has some other strong pattern can take up the slack and the firm will grow. When there is no such partner, however, the venture typically does not do well at all. Usually it is overmanaged. It may be managed to death.

When a venture has completed the early stages of growth and has enough employees to be managed, a Real Manager can be of considerable help. This pattern also helps with established firms—family businesses and companies that are purchased. Corporate ventures can benefit from a Real Manager in charge, as can ventures capitalized well enough to be big from day one.

If you are a Real Manager, this pattern can help you to be a successful entrepreneur only when there is enough of an organization present to need managing. Otherwise, being a Real Manager does not help you to achieve entrepreneurial success; it can in fact hurt you.

WHAT MAKES A REAL MANAGER

Real Managers may possess up to six characteristics.[2] The mix can vary from person to person, but a Real Manager will have at least half of these six characteristics:

1. Desire to be a corporate leader
2. Decisiveness
3. Positive attitudes to authority
4. Desire to compete
5. Desire for power
6. Desire to stand out from the crowd

Desire to Be a Corporate Leader

Real Managers want to climb the ladder of occupational success, and they view attaining the upper rungs of that ladder as a very good thing. Placed in any large organization, they immediately look upward, because top management is their goal.

Closely related to this desire for occupational upward mobility is a desire to find opportunities to fully utilize their talents. These individuals wish to be creative by using their capabilities and feel strongly that those capabilities should not be left unfulfilled. Furthermore, they must utilize their talents in something worthwhile—such as moving up the corporate ladder.

Because of their strong drive to assume corporate leadership positions, Real Managers perform well in these positions and develop considerable self-assurance as a result. They believe they are effective in dealing with problems that confront them. They have faith in their own abilities. Furthermore, they develop a capacity to direct and coordinate the work of others so as to organize and integrate activities in pursuit of mutual goals. This too contributes to self-confidence.

As a result, Real Managers feel very secure. They are so confident in their talents that they are entirely unworried about how an employer may deal with them, and they are unconcerned about such things as employment continuity.

Desire to be a corporate leader is a bundle of motives organized around the need to move up the corporate ladder and occupy a position at or near the top. Even in a small firm, to fully satisfy the Real Manager, some type of hierarchy or occupational ladder must exist.

Decisiveness

Real Managers are decisive people who are quick and self-assured decision makers. If a decision must be made, they go ahead and make it. Real Managers believe that it is better to make a decision than to beg the issue; to them ascertaining all the facts about an issue is almost impossible, and therefore action now is the best course. Hesitation may mean that currently minor problems become major ones. Decisiveness is not entirely independent of a desire to be a corporate leader, but it focuses on the decision-making aspects of managerial work.

Positive Attitudes to Authority

Managers are typically expected to behave in ways that do not provoke negative reactions from their superiors; ideally they elicit positive reactions. Managers must represent their groups upward in the organization and obtain support for their actions at higher levels. This requires a good relationship between manager and superior.

Thus Real Managers have a generally positive attitude toward those holding positions of authority over them. They like and respect their bosses; thus it is much easier to work with them in the numerous instances where cooperative efforts are needed.

In contrast, any tendency to generalized hatred, distaste, or anxiety in dealing with people in positions of authority makes it extremely difficult to meet managerial job demands. Relations with superiors are either minimal or filled with so much negative feeling that communication is hampered. Corporations require communication up and down a managerial hierarchy of authority; negative attitudes to authority block that process.

Desire to Compete

At least insofar as managers at the same level are concerned, a strong competitive aspect is built into their work. This occurs because of the pyramid-like nature of organizations, with fewer and fewer positions to compete for as the manager ascends the corporate ladder. As a result, somebody wins and somebody loses. If managers do not compete, they may lose ground as they and their functions are relegated to lower and lower status levels. Without competitive behavior, promotion is unlikely.

Real Managers characteristically strive to win for themselves and their units and accept such challenges as other managers at a comparable level may introduce. On occasion challenges come from below, from among subordinates. To meet all these competitive challenges, managers must like to compete, and the best managers enjoy rivalry of this kind and are motivated to seek it out whenever possible. Being unwilling to fight for position, status, advancement, and ideas almost certainly brings failure. Such a manager may be ignored so consistently that the whole unit disappears from the organization chart or is merged into or subordinated to some other unit. If a person tends to associate unpleasant emotions, such as anxiety and depression, with competition, that person almost surely behaves ineffectively or withdraws from the competition entirely.

Although this competitive behavior may take a variety of forms, assertiveness in dealing with others is certainly an important feature. Assertiveness training is widely sponsored by companies to improve managerial effectiveness. Real Managers are assertive by nature. They do not lie back and wait for the action to come to them. They push forward and express their views; they are proactive rather than reactive. To the extent the situation requires it, they take charge, push decisions, establish discipline, and protect others for whom they feel responsible. This is how they compete.

Desire for Power

It is the nature of larger organizations that their managers not only relate to others above them (involving attitudes to authority) and to people at the same level (involving competitiveness), but also downward, to people below them on the ladder. In this relationship exercising power is often required to structure the work and get people to perform as expected. When this becomes necessary, Real Managers must tell those below them what to do. They must enforce their words with an appropriate use of rewards and punishments. An individual who finds this difficult and emotionally disturbing, who does not wish to impose on others or believes it is wrong to utilize power, is not going to perform well in this particular situation. On the other hand a favorable attitude toward using power, perhaps even enjoyment in exercising it appropriately, contributes to successful performance as a manager.

Real Managers to whom the exercise of power comes naturally tend to have a practical orientation. They emphasize the "here and now"; use data that focus on specific facts; are action oriented; and look for speed, efficiency, and results. They tend to have the drive and energy needed to accomplish difficult tasks.

Real Managers who like using power give particular attention to facts, rules, and procedures. Ambiguity and a lack of structure are not attractive to them, with the result that they try to reduce both. Short fact-filled communications are preferred. As managers, they are impersonal, forceful, and often dislike committees and group decision making. The risk is that they can be too structured and may simplify a situation too much. Yet overall they make good managers.

Desire to Stand Out from the Crowd

Being a manager requires acting differently from other people. Real Managers must stand out from their group and assume a position of high visibility. They cannot use the actions of their subordinates as guides for their own behavior. Instead they are called on to deviate from the immediate group and to do things that inevitably invite attention, discussion, and perhaps even criticism from those who report to them. Being a manager requires assuming a position of considerable importance insofar as the motives and emotions of other people are concerned. When this prospect is viewed as unattractive, when the idea of standing out from the crowd and being highly visible creates discomfort, it is hard to be a good manager. If a manager enjoys being at the center of attention and prefers to deviate somewhat from others, it is easier to manage well. Such a person often has many of the characteristics of a good actor. Certainly managers are frequently "on stage" and are expected to follow scripts that differ substantially from those of many around them.

Often these "scripts" call for carrying out a number of administrative duties that are strictly managerial in nature: communicating and making the decisions in a responsible manner. Real Managers must at least be willing to face these activities and, ideally, they gain some satisfaction from carrying them out. Again, if standing out in this manner is consistently viewed with apprehension or loathing, the chances of success in management would appear to be considerably less. A desire to put off or avoid the more or less standard managerial duties can result in an irresponsible manager.

WHAT REAL MANAGERS LOOK LIKE

Note that running through the characteristics of Real Managers is the idea that a chain of command, or managerial hierarchy, or occupational ladder exists in the company. If that is not true, managing is not relevant. In many small entrepreneurial firms this kind of managerial ladder exists to only a minimal degree, if that. To understand the Real Manager entrepreneur it is important, therefore, not only to recognize the type of person, but to recognize the environments in which that person will thrive. Many of these occur in large corporations. Much fewer occur within entrepreneurship.

With this in mind I consider two very successful Real Manager entrepreneurs—Paul Shine of AIM Corrugated Container Corporation, a family business, and Jerome Schentag of the Pharmacokinetics Laboratory of Millard Fillmore Hospital, a joint corporate venture.

Paul Shine at AIM Corrugated Container Corporation

AIM is a second-generation family business with Paul Shine as its president and Kevin Shine as its vice president of operations. Paul was an accountant previously with Arthur Andersen, and Kevin had a law practice. It has been only a few years since control shifted from the father to the sons.

The business was started to sell surplus and misprinted boxes. It now manufactures corrugated boxes, displays, signs, and other products from sheets of corrugated board that it purchases. It markets within a 150-mile radius of the Buffalo plant, selling primarily to the furniture, printing, food service, and metal manufacturing industries.

The plant itself is technologically advanced and highly computerized. Flat sheets are cut, creased, slotted, and folded by machine and then glued, taped, stitched, and printed as needed. Much of the work is customized. The major competitive advantage is in high-quality products and in service that provides for delivery times well below the industry average. The company has its own trucks to expedite delivery.

AIM operates in a very competitive industry and has been hurt by the closing of manufacturing plants as a result of the business downturn in its market area. Nevertheless there has been steady growth in sales—to $7 million a year currently—and in the number of employees—to 55. Recently in particular there has been substantial sales growth, after several years at a plateau. The firm has been profitable in every year but its first and has provided a comfortable income to the Shine family over the years.

Paul Shine is above the average for established entrepreneurs as both a Personal Achiever and a Supersalesperson. But his really pronounced entrepreneurial strength is as a Real Manager. He is a directive manager, which means he focuses on facts and prefers structure, is action oriented, decisive, and looks for speed, efficiency, and results. Accomplishing difficult tasks and exercising power and control come easily to such people. They are not always comfortable with this style but they tend to use it, and very effectively. Shine is highly competitive; he wants to win and drives hard to get his company to the top. He tends to structure the work of those who report to him, giving them a clear picture of what he expects. Although it is sometimes difficult to do so, he can take charge and put pressure on those who do not perform. These are the signs of a good manager and are entirely consistent with his position as president of the company. They also fit with the kind of person who tends to manage the sales process.

This pattern is reflected in the test results:

Desire to be a corporate leader	*High*
Decisiveness	*Not a Factor*
Positive attitudes to authority	*Not a Factor*
Desire to compete	*High*
Desire for power	*Very High*
Desire to stand out from the crowd	*Not a Factor*

As a Real Manager and to a much lesser degree a Supersalesman as well, it is not surprising that Shine has devoted his talents heavily to the sales and marketing aspects of the business in recent years. He handles a number of accounts himself simply because these are people who have become used to dealing with him, but he keeps on top of what his sales staff is doing as well. Much of the process of negotiating prices falls to him. Although his brother Kevin now handles the operations end, he set up many of the systems there originally. The two have worked together to continue the rapid delivery and high-quality service that have given AIM its competitive advantage over the years. This has paid off in that the company is able to position itself at a price level that permits an entirely adequate profit margin. There are problems in that the expensive equipment could be run for longer hours and the sales staff could be utilized more effectively, but Shine is working on these. The company is growing once again and it is making money. There is every reason to believe that company growth will be managed into the future just as it has been in the past.

Jerome Schentag at the Pharmacokinetics Laboratory of Millard Fillmore Hospital

The Pharmacokinetics Laboratory of Millard Fillmore Hospital does multidisciplinary research and development in the fields of pharmaceutics and clinical pharmacology. Most of its income comes from grants and contracts with government agencies, foundations, and in particular business firms. It also has some income from its two owners, the hospital where it is situated and the State University of New York at Buffalo. The former represents payment for consultations and therapeutic drug monitoring. The latter supports faculty members and their teaching activities in pharmacy and medicine. The professional staff consists of pharmacists, physicians, and nurses primarily, but the laboratory has diversified into other areas including computer systems, analytical chemistry, engineering, and epidemiology to protect against downturns in drug development cycles. Although originally most of the work was done for government, it has now shifted heavily to industry.

Growth has been quite rapid, approaching 40 percent a year. Sales now amount to $3.5 million a year and there are 68 employees. Since this is a nonprofit organization, there are strictly speaking no profits. What might be construed as profit is put back into the laboratory to purchase new equipment. This in turn permits it to remain competitive in a context where new laboratories are sprouting up constantly. It is not uncommon for these competitors to be headed by professionals who honed their skills originally in Buffalo.

Although he is an Expert Idea Generator to a degree as his professional activities would suggest and an above average Personal Achiever as well, Schentag emerges as first and foremost a Real Manager. He relates well to those in authority over him, and such people exist in both the university and hospital hierarchies. Overall he has a generally favorable predisposition to those who hold such authority, and thus he finds it easy to communicate with them. He is very competitive, and as a result winning is important to him. Peers, both outside and within his organization, can incite his competitive juices and get him going. Losing is not something he likes at all. Not surprisingly he can be assertive and outspoken as well. We have found that many good teachers and those who attract attention in an organization often like to stand out from the group and be the center of attention. Schentag has this quality. He is also highly motivated to get routine managerial tasks done. He does not leave things uncompleted; he is on top of his work at all times.

All this makes for a very good manager, but there is more. He has a great deal of self-assurance, with the result that he believes in himself and projects that image to others. Decisions come easily to him and he is very secure in the knowledge he brings to his work. Work is in fact fun for him; it gives him an opportunity to use his talents and be himself. Schentag is constantly reaching out to deal with new challenges. There is no sense in which the demands of his job overwhelm him.

These characteristics are reflected in his Real Manager pattern:

Desire to be a corporate leader	*High*
Decisiveness	*High*
Positive attitudes to authority	*High*
Desire to compete	*Very High*
Desire for power	*Not a Factor*
Desire to stand out from the crowd	*Very High*

Schentag has headed his organization for well over 10 years, during the period of its most rapid growth. He has a doctorate in clinical pharmacy from Philadelphia College of Pharmacy and Science. He is a full professor in the School of Pharmacy at the State University of New York at Buffalo, publishes extensively in the professional literature, serves on numerous committees at both the university and the hospital, and is active in a number of different professional associations. In addition to managing the laboratory and having ultimate responsibility for paying the bills, he is also personally involved in sales, handling the larger contracts.

This is a really difficult managerial job. Being a renowned scientist helps, but it is far from a total solution. There are competing demands from the university for pure research and from the hospital for patient care. Scientists have big egos and can be difficult to deal with. They are needed to do research, but the better they are the more they are in demand by competing laboratories. Keeping them happy is not always an easy job. Schentag has a number of group leaders reporting to him who become increasingly adept at raising money. Retaining them beyond five years is a monumental task. Furthermore, there are demands from contractors that must constantly be dealt with. Conflict is everywhere, managerial power is often short-lived, and negotiation is a constant way of life. Balancing income with payment demands can be a tricky matter of timing. Simply holding the organization together is an accomplishment. Growing it in the way that it has is an outstanding managerial feat. Schentag came to management with strong motivation, but some uncertainty regarding his skills. After all, he was basically a scientist and a professor. Experience has now worked wonders—he is indeed a Real Manager, and in a highly entrepreneurial context.

CONCLUSION

Like Supersalespeople, Real Managers can have very successful careers without ever going near an entrepreneurial venture. Also it is important to recognize that although managing is their forte and the way that Real Managers can contribute most to their ventures, they have a strength in a certain kind of managed selling as well.

Real Managers can be recognized by their possession of many of the following characteristics:

1. Desire to be a corporate leader
2. Decisiveness
3. Positive attitudes to authority
4. Desire to compete
5. Desire for power
6. Desire to stand out from the crowd

Underlying all of these characteristics is the expectation that the company is large enough, and so structured, that a number of levels of management exist and management skills can be fully utilized. In addition, whether you should enter on a career in entrepreneurship if you are a Real Manager depends on what other strong patterns you possess, what you have learned thus far in life, what opportunities you can identify, and where your career has taken you to date. This perspective of Real Managers will be discussed further in Chapter 6.

NOTES

1. We present our research dealing with this finding in three articles—one with Frederic E. Berman in *Personnel Psychology*, one with Norman R. Smith in *Strategic Management Journal*, and one by myself only in the *Journal of Business Venturing*.
2. These characteristics derive from research that compares the personalities of more and less effective corporate managers. This research is described in *Explorations in Managerial Talent* by Edwin E. Ghiselli, in *Managing with Style* by Alan J. Rowe and Richard O. Mason, and in my book *Role Motivation Theories*.

CHAPTER 6

How Real Managers Succeed or Fail

The description of the Real Manager in Chapter 5 matches closely the personality patterns of effective and successful managers in many large corporations. Now, however, we need to look at how these people can achieve successful careers as entrepreneurs. If you are a Real Manager, how should you follow the Managing Route to entrepreneurial success, and what are the traps to avoid along the way?

THE MANAGING ROUTE

Real Managers enjoy playing a leadership role. They often begin taking on that role at an early age, becoming officers and captains of organizations and teams when they are in school. And not uncommonly Real Managers pursue a managerial career in a large organization for some time prior to becoming entrepreneurs. Unlike Personal Achievers, this is done not for training purposes, but as a career in and of itself. Often the move into entrepreneurship is prompted by a major opportunity that presents itself, or when a strictly corporate managerial career runs into difficulties. In recent years, as large corporations have faced substantial downsizing, many good managers have found themselves unemployed. Starting a business under these latter circumstances can provide a solution. It depends on the person, and on the nature of the entrepreneurial situation.

Following the Managing Route is simply a matter of being yourself and doing what comes naturally. There are two ways of doing this as an entrepreneur:

1. You can manage your own employees, if there are a sufficient number of employees, and more than one level of management so that some organization structure exists.
2. You can manage people outside your organization into buying the products or services of your firm. This activity is particularly attractive when your firm is small and there is little opportunity to manage internally.

To follow this first approach to the Managing Route within entrepreneurship, the Real Manager must find or start a venture large enough to utilize managerial skills. The Managing Route is activated as a company grows, to avoid "hitting the wall," as described in Chapter 2.[1] Being a Real Manager is also valuable to people pursuing a career in corporate venturing. It helps in bridging the cultural gap between corporate management and venture operations.[2] Not surprisingly, Real Managers can make the transition to company management rather easily should they sell their firm and accept an employment contract with the purchaser. Personal Achievers, in contrast, often have considerable difficulty with this type of transition.

Once established in a venture of some size, the Real Manager brings to an organization a capacity to manage it into substantial growth. Standardized procedures are introduced, the organizational structure is stabilized, managers are developed, and systems are put in place. This is the Managing Route in entrepreneurship. It is the process of institutionalizing a venture. Real Managers are very good at this, and if ventures are to grow beyond the small business category, they absolutely need Real Managers following the Managing Route.

In the other approach to the Managing Route, Real Managers can be effective in sales occupations. I find that within a particular company the sales managers often exhibit the strongest managerial patterns. This tie between managing and sales appears to occur because both managing and selling involve influencing other people to do what you wish. A manager often can bring more authority to bear in this process, but in certain situations, a salesperson has substantial leverage. Reciprocity situations, for instance, almost require that a buyer purchase from a particular source.

In any event Real Managers can be very effective at selling, if they can manage people into buying their product or service. They certainly do not sell in the same way as Supersalespeople, and not all Real Managers are attracted to selling. Yet if an attraction does develop, they can bring their managerial skills to bear in the sales process so as to achieve considerable success.

These two approaches to the Managing Route are well illustrated in the case of Daniel Blatz. Blatz is a strong Real Manager who has followed the Managing Route closely in both its managing and selling aspects. As a result his firm has enjoyed a great deal of success.

Daniel Blatz of Supplemental Health Care Services

Supplemental Health Care Services was started by Leo Blatz, Daniel's brother, and Leo's wife Laurie, both of whom are nurses, as a per diem nursing agency to provide temporary services to hospitals and nursing homes in Western New York. It continues to concentrate on the placement of nurses, but now includes physicians, dentists, hospital administrators, and a wide range of paramedical personnel as well. Services provided include recruitment, interviews, reference and licensure verification, visa processing, transportation arrangement, and predeparture orientation. Personnel are sent under contract to work stations throughout the United States and in Canada, Australia, Egypt, Saudi Arabia, and China. Placements extend from three months to a year or more. A small percentage of the business involves permanent placement of medical personnel overseas and providing expert witnesses and legal consultations.

Supplemental Health Care Services has some 600 employees over the course of a year. There is a small corporate office in Buffalo, and several other offices within the United States. Yearly income is now approaching $10 million and in spite of declines in the industry as a whole, company profits have remained good.

Daniel Blatz has the title of contract administrator. He secures government contracts, establishes labor rates and benefits, handles company advertising, deals with government compliance matters such as affirmative action, and does purchasing. Approximately 100 bids are submitted each year. Blatz is a graduate of the State University of New York at Buffalo in business administration and has worked as a manager for several firms.

He is indeed a Personal Achiever in the more typical entrepreneurial sense, but even more he is a Real Manager. Working with others who have authority over him comes easily; he is typically favorably disposed toward these people and understands the problems they face. He is also good at making presentations to groups and accepting a role as the center of attention. The managerial role is different, and he not only understands that fact but is comfortable with it and even enjoys it. Sometimes managers need to be something of an actor, as if they were on stage. Blatz takes well to that type of role.

Another managerial characteristic is perceiving oneself as effective in dealing with problems that arise, as sound in judgment and capable of coping with challenging situations. Blatz has this type of belief in himself, which permits him to deal with new circumstances that others might back away from. He is confident in his own talents and secure in his work. This is not the kind of person who is fearful of losing his job or of being taken advantage of by his employer. He works because he finds what he does interesting, not out of a fear of failure.

Blatz is good at making decisions; he is a ready, quick, and self-confident decision maker. When a decision needs to be made, he recognizes the fact and moves ahead. Although it is desirable to have as much information as possible, it is also true that hesitation can result in a closing of the window of opportunity. That is something he rarely lets happen.

As a Real Manager, Blatz's personality constellation looks as follows:

Desire to be a corporate leader	*High*
Decisiveness	*Very High*
Positive attitudes to authority	*Very High*
Desire to compete	*Not a Factor*
Desire for power	*Not a Factor*
Desire to stand out from the crowd	*High*

These are qualities that make for an effective manager. Outside of work Blatz referees various types of sports events, and his managerial strengths are clearly manifest in that context. But they pay off even more in his job. Although he reports to his brother, he is in fact free to make most of his own decisions and run things as he sees fit. That is the way he likes it, and it brings out the best in him. He formulated and implemented a marketing plan that raised his division's earnings from under $3 million to $7.5 million in two years. In that time period 25 percent of the competition went out of business. The growth of the contract business, in contradistinction to the original per diem nursing business in Western New York, is almost entirely a consequence of his managerial talents. He is an expert at putting bids together because he knows when to stop collecting data and go with what he has. There are times when he misses, but this is far from being the norm. On occasion the people he places do not work out, and it becomes necessary to replace them. Blatz can do that. He is constantly concerned with finding methods of motivating people so as to manage his operation more effectively. Certainly it has been a major success.

GETTING STARTED ON
THE MANAGING ROUTE

Real Managers may come to their firms in a variety of ways, much the same as with other entrepreneurial types. Table 5 shows the starting point for the 33 Real Managers among the 100 established entrepreneurs in Western New York whom I studied.

Real Managers prefer to start firms, and in particular, they start them without partners. This appears at first glance to be in conflict with what I said previously; if Real Managers tend to overmanage small firms with few employees, start-ups by Real Managers should rarely be found among a group of well-established firms such as these, because most would have been managed into the ground long before.

I find, however, few ventures among these start-ups that are headed by people who are Real Managers and Real Managers only. In most cases other patterns are present as well. (Chapter 9 discusses in depth "complex" or multiple-pattern entrepreneurs.) In particular these Real Managers who started firms tend to be Personal Achievers in addition. This multiple pattern works very well in start-ups, and apparently its presence serves to cancel out the tendency to overmanage.

Even though 24 percent of the Real Managers took over family businesses, this figure is close to what I found among the entrepreneurs who did not show any strong pattern. Note that Real Managers are unlikely to start a sales or professional practice where dedication to growth is minimal or nonexistent. They want something large enough to manage. This is consistent with the elevated figures in Table 5 for some type of corporate venturing. Corporate ventures provide a good way to follow the Managing Route.

SUCCESS ON THE MANAGING ROUTE

Table 6 shows that Real Managers on the Managing Route can be very successful in growing a business. Unlike Supersalespeople, Real Managers do not suffer severely during recession. This is probably because their ventures are bigger. Also they are unlikely to have firms that barely survive. When that does happen it is because a small firm is controlled by a Real Manager, who lacks another strong pattern or a partner to buffer the impact of overmanaging.

Table 5   HOW REAL MANAGERS
BECOME ENTREPRENEURS

Started Firm Without Partners	28%
Started Firm with Partners	18
Purchased Firm	12
Took Over Family Firm	24
Initiated Corporate Venture	9
Was Turnaround Person in Corporate Venture	6
Started Sales or Professional Practice	3
Total	100%

Table 6   HOW THE REAL MANAGERS'
FIRMS SUCCEEDED

Entrepreneur and Firm Stayed Together	
Firm Has Grown a Lot	43%
Firm Has Grown Some	21
Recession Has Hurt Firm	3
Firm Has Only Survived	3
Entrepreneur and Firm No Longer Together	
Left Firm and Started New Venture	9
Left Firm and Had Nonentrepreneurial Career Subsequently	3
Insufficient Information Available	18
Total	100%

Two aspects of the Managing Route can prove difficult to understand, and I want to give you a better picture of these. One involves how a Real Manager can achieve success even though the firm is small. Gary Posluszny's case gives some good insights here. Second is the ease with which Real Managers can move back and forth between entrepreneurship and the corporate world, unlike Personal Achievers for instance. Robert Miller provides a nice example of how this can work.

Gary Posluszny of K.D.M. Die Company

K.D.M. started as a result of a plant closing when three separated employees combined their skills to start the company. Shortly afterward, Posluszny and his father joined this group and ultimately came to own the small company. On the father's retirement, Gary and his brother Carl took over. K.D.M. is now operated by a very closely knit family. It provides drop forge dies, tool and die operations, and tool and cutter manufacture to a limited set of customers. The work is highly skilled.

The firm has grown steadily over the years and annual sales now total $700,000. Employment levels have fluctuated between 10 and 15 in recent years, but a major factor here has been the introduction of computerized technology which reduced the need for personnel. The company, although highly technologically capable, is positioned in a declining industry. That it has been able to grow and earn a profit while putting money back into the business is indicative of its inherent strength.

Posluszny is a Personal Achiever consistent with the entrepreneurial origins of the firm, but even more he is a Real Manager. What he has really done is to manage the technology and skilled personnel of the company into a pattern of slow but steady growth. His style is characterized by a practical orientation, a focus on the here and now, and a concern for action and efficiency. He gets things done and focuses on problems internal to his firm. Technical skills, operating procedures, and results are important to him. He is a good supervisor who clearly establishes what he wants done. Furthermore, he does not leave things to chance. He works hard, sees that routine matters are carried out, and assures himself that the work gets done in a timely manner. Although it is his direct supervisory capability in dealing with immediate subordinates that is most in evidence, Posluszny is also president of his company, and that is no accident. He has a great deal of self-assurance in dealing with the problems that confront him. He knows his business, its skills, and its technology, and he is secure in that knowledge. His family background and work culture provide him with a great deal of strength.

Posluszny's most pronounced Real Manager characteristic is his desire for power, but he possesses other managerial capabilities as well.

Desire to be a corporate leader	*High*
Decisiveness	*Not a Factor*
Positive attitudes to authority	*Not a Factor*
Desire to compete	*Not a Factor*
Desire for power	*Very High*
Desire to stand out from the crowd	*High*

Although in recent years Posluszny has delegated much control over day-to-day-operations to his brother, he remains involved. A key to the company's success is that it has taken young people directly out of high school and trained them to do highly skilled work. In this way costs are kept down and it is possible to obtain unusually capable people. Management places quality above everything else and this quality is achieved through hands-on, direct training of the young workers.

Posluszny trains, he establishes goals, and he is beginning to focus more on producing high-profit-margin items and competitor analysis. Equipment has been continuously modernized and the people to operate it have been well trained. The skilled workers are highly competent, they can quote jobs, but they cannot manage. That job falls to the Posluszny brothers. They have managed K.D.M. through major changes. The product has gone from relatively simple/shallow parts to very complex and medium-depth parts. Technological quality from both people and machines has become increasingly important. That requires constant attention from management. The company is not growing rapidly, but its progress is steady and it is very well managed. That is why it remains in existence in an industry where many firms have failed. Posluszny is now giving increasing attention to the sales and marketing end of the business with a view to managing it into more rapid growth.

Robert Miller of MPC Health Care Services and Fay's Drug Stores

MPC Health Care Services started as a retail community pharmacy. Over the years it went though a number of changes both in its business activities and in the locations served. Ultimately the retail end was sold. What remained was a company providing pharmacy services to the frail elderly, terminally ill, and cognitively impaired residing in long-term care facilities. Primarily this is a service to nursing homes, although MPC also serves prisons and facilities for the mentally retarded. The company has three divisions, the largest of which is involved in dispensing drugs to long-term care facilities. Another division provides nutrients to patients who cannot be fed orally. There is also a consulting division that introduces clinical skills of a pharmaceutical nature to nursing homes under various federal and state mandates.

Except for some problems in the early years, which resulted in the shakeout of a partner, MPC Health Care Services has grown steadily in its dollar volume of sales and in retained earnings. When the retail business was sold, sales did drop, but even this loss was recovered shortly afterward. Most recently the company has $3.6 million in annual sales and 38 employees. There are 32 clients and 3,200 nursing home beds served. This has been a growing and consistently profitable business over a long period of time.

Very recently the assets of MPC Health Care Services were sold to Fay's Drug Stores, thus creating a regional managed pharmacy services division, which with two other acquisitions now has some $32 million a year in sales statewide. Fay's, which is diversified into other retail areas as well, is a publicly held company with over $1 billion in annual sales. The whole industry has been consolidating, and this is but part of the process.

Miller started MPC many years ago and now as a result of the sale is a Fay's Drug executive. The predominant pattern in his psychological profile is that of Real Manager. No other factor is nearly as strong. He takes charge of things and assures himself that operations are carried out efficiently and without error. That is important in the business he is in. He is oriented toward action and is decisive. Facts, rules, and procedures are of major concern to him and he likes to establish standardized systems. He has no problem standing out from others and assuming highly visible positions. He likes to lead and plays the leadership role well. Things are not left to chance. Decisions that need to be made are made. Memos that need to be written are written. People who need to be contacted are contacted. There is in all this a considerable degree of self-assurance. Miller believes in his ability to handle problems and make correct decisions. He likes to wield power. Yet he does this with an understanding of his impact on others and a considerable amount of tact. One of his greatest strengths is that he is not afraid to ask questions when things are not going as well as they should. Furthermore, he can share power with others if he feels that is the way to get a job done well. If an activity is not being carried out effectively, he will take action to correct the situation.

Miller's strengths as a Real Manager are pronounced.

Desire to be a corporate leader	*High*
Decisiveness	*High*
Positive attitudes to authority	*Not a Factor*
Desire to compete	*Not a Factor*
Desire for power	*Very High*
Desire to stand out from the crowd	*Very High*

Before starting MPC Health Care Services, Miller worked as a manager for several drugstore operations. His approach with his own business was to manage steady growth, watching for problems and opportunities, keeping errors to an absolute minimum, and introducing standardized procedures and systems whenever possible. He tried hard to stay ahead of the competition and generally succeeded. At the time of the sale to Fay's, he believed that certain industry trends were operating to force consolidation and give major advantages to the larger companies. Selling was simply the practical thing to do. Since the sale, Miller has operated as a regional account executive for Fay's under an employment contract negotiated at the time of the sale. He manages a number of accounts that he brought with him, and he enjoys the work fully.

Miller sold many of these accounts originally. He presents himself to clients as a person who knows his profession and will be sure that things get done right. Errors are the worst thing that can happen in the pharmacy business, and he clearly is not one to let errors occur if he can help it. Clients have faith in his judgment. In addition to his managerial job, Miller teaches in the State University of New York at Buffalo School of Pharmacy and is active in executive positions within his professional association. The transition from his own business to Fay's has been relatively easy. He continues to look for opportunities to manage in the future; at this point he is happy where he is but is not entirely sure that he wants ultimately to retire from that position.

Note that Posluszny has delegated much of the managing to his brother, who is also a partner. He is devoting increasing amounts of time to the sales aspects of the business, thus "managing outward" more. Finally, he is a Personal Achiever in addition to being a Real Manager. That makes it easier to accept some ambiguity and be flexible. You clearly can be a Real Manager and still not overmanage a rather small business. Yet the possibility of overmanaging should be a constant concern.

Miller was a manager in several businesses before forming MPC Health Care. He then managed MPC into major growth, and he made the transition to Fay's Drug Stores with ease. The moral: If you are a Real Manager, you can go back and forth between the corporate and entrepreneurial worlds as the realities of the situation require it. You remain on the Managing Route.

AVOIDING THE TRAPS
ALONG THE MANAGING ROUTE

Like any route the Managing Route has its share of traps that you need to avoid.

The Real Manager Lacks the Needed Knowledge and Skills

The Real Manager–Managing Route fit can go wrong because entrepreneurial managers move too quickly into managing on their own. They do not yet know what they are doing. Managers, even highly motivated and talented managers, need to know how to manage. If Real Managers do not learn this—and there is a substantial knowledge component here—they are not going to achieve the necessary fit with the Managing Route. A major problem is that if you have never managed, it is very difficult to achieve the requisite skills; in most cases you have to learn managing while doing it.[3] Management training programs and some MBA programs often try to teach managing to people who have never managed. The results can be catastrophic.

The antidote: Take time to learn. There are various ways to learn management; the best way is to manage for someone else for a while. Dan Blatz of Supplemental Health Care Services and Bob Miller of MPC Health Care Services managed in other companies before moving into their own ventures. Gary Posluszny of K.D.M. Die Company managed under his father's tutelage before he became president. I believe you need good role models to become a good manager. Find one and learn.

The Real Manager Overmanages a Small Venture

A problem also arises when entrepreneurs try to manage ventures that are still too small. Building a substantial amount of structure and using highly standardized systems in very small firms can yield major problems; the Achieving Route (with its informal, unstructured approach) is preferred. If the Real Manager has a partner with complementary talents or if the Real Manager has a supplementary pattern such as Personal Achiever, this can help to head off this problem. But without these, Real Managers tend to manage very small firms into either failure or bare survival, simply because the firms are not yet ready for their particular talents.

The antidote: Pick your opportunities. If you are a Real Manager only or are the kind of person who really wants to put his or her managerial talents to work, find a venture that is large enough to manage. The answer may be in corporate venturing or purchasing an established firm or taking over a family business. It may even be in participating in a large-scale start-up. The key: Before jumping into entrepreneurship, be absolutely sure there is something there to manage, and thus that following the Managing Route is possible.

The Real Manager Strays Off the Managing Route

When firms are large enough to be managed, and the Managing Route is appropriate for Real Managers, you can still go astray. One trap: Real

Managers who have established an affinity for selling continue down the Selling Route, when a delicate shift from managing customers to managing employees would contribute more to the firm, given its current state of growth. Normally people with managerial potential like to manage and will seek it out. This is not, however, always true among the inexperienced, who have not yet learned to tie their managerial yearnings to actual managerial work. Thus Real Managers may strive for some other use of their talents than managing. The alignment can go wrong, with the result that they attempt to become a Supersalesperson or a Personal Achiever, or an Expert Idea Generator (which they are not), and thus go astray.

The antidote: If you do not yet know that managing is the career for you, explore opportunities and open yourself up to new experiences. Give yourself a chance to learn what kind of a person you are and where you do the best work. If you are a Real Manager, you will come to know it.

There are traps awaiting, however, as companies continue to grow under the impetus of a Real Manager. There comes a time when this trajectory leads to a strategy that is best described as technical tinkering—it leads to goals that move very close to impossible perfection, to an organizational culture that is technocratically dominated, and to a highly rigid structure.[4] As a result, the potential for adjustment to environmental change is lost, and the firm becomes at risk. After many years heavily managed firms can lose the capacity for adapting to change; this is not always true, and it is certainly not something to worry about in the early years, but it can pose a threat later on.

A major factor is whether the company has accumulated extensive knowledge of its industry and thus the capacity to predict change. When Real Managers continue to keep on top of their technologies, their markets, and changes in their human resource bases they do not get caught in this focusing trajectory; they can and do adapt. Thus an important antidote for the Real Manager is to stay sufficiently attentive to the environment outside the company, to learn new things, and to run the business in such a way as to be continually ready for change.

CONCLUSION

To be successful, Real Managers must stay on the Managing Route in a firm large enough to need managing. They may turn their managerial talents to the sales process, and thus exert influence externally with customers, as well as internally with employees. The Managing Route may involve performing both of these activities or only one.

Traps along the Managing Route include:

1. A Real Manager fails to accumulate the knowledge needed to manage well and the skills needed to convert this talent into action.
2. A Real Manager overmanages or micro-manages a small venture with few employees, thus stifling the venture.
3. A Real Manager strays off the Managing Route either out of a failure to understand that managing provides the best fit for his or her talents, or because circumstances convince a person that some other route is more appropriate.

Often the Managing Route involves taking over after a Personal Achiever has "hit the wall," thus permitting a company to keep on growing. That Personal Achiever may be the Real Manager if he or she is lucky enough to possess both patterns, or the Real Manager may be another entrepreneur. Either way, there is plenty of room within entrepreneurship for Real Managers to exercise their talents.

NOTES

1. A good discussion of this shift to a managed structure as a firm grows is contained in an article by Neil C. Churchill and Virginia L. Lewis in the *Harvard Business Review*.
2. This gap is discussed in detail in the book by Zenas Block and Ian C. MacMillan titled *Corporate Venturing*.
3. My work on how managers cope with ineffective performance in subordinates is presented in *People Problems*.
4. Again I draw on Danny Miller's treatment in *The Icarus Paradox*.

CHAPTER 7

The Expert
Idea Generator
Entrepreneur

Expert Idea Generators are people who have ideas for a business that can provide a real competitive advantage. Expert Idea Generators may be merely innovative: they find an idea and see opportunity in introducing it in a new situation. Many, however, are really creative: they come up with an idea that is truly original with them.[1]

Under the best of circumstances Expert Idea Generators act effectively on these ideas and follow the Idea Generating Route to success. If you are an Expert Idea Generator, you may be an inventor who thinks up new products and pursues their development. You may be heavily involved in the world of high technology. Yet the ideas of Expert Idea Generators may also involve market niches, approaches to obtaining a competitive advantage, innovations in administrative processes, or any other idea that gives an edge over other businesses.

This chapter describes these Expert Idea Generators and provides several examples of such people. In Chapter 8 I take up the ways that Expert Idea Generators can best utilize their talents and follow the Idea Generating Route. My goal in both chapters is to give you an understanding of how people who are good at developing ideas achieve success as entrepreneurs.

WHAT MAKES AN
EXPERT IDEA GENERATOR

In many cases Expert Idea Generators become tremendously enthused about their ideas and devote a great deal of energy to implementing them. Unlike Personal Achievers, however, who devote huge amounts of energy to the venture as a whole, Expert Idea Generators focus their energy more narrowly on the idea itself. If the idea fails and the venture moves off in other directions, they tend to lose interest. Sometimes their energies are focused primarily on persuading others to contribute to implementing what they have created; the emphasis is on raising capital, getting others involved, obtaining government support, and the like. Expert Idea Generators may or may not be strong on personal follow-through. If their ideas are so compelling, or their persuasion so effective, others may join the venture. And this can work as well as when the Expert Idea Generator invests a great deal of personal energy to implement the ideas. However, someone must carry the Expert Idea Generating torch on down the route to entrepreneurial success—implementation must match idea generation.

Not infrequently the ventures of Expert Idea Generators start out within corporations: The result may be a wholly owned corporate venture, or a spinoff of a venture, or an independent breakaway. In the high technology area in particular, large capital needs and the importance of technological backing may foster considerable early corporate or government involvement.[2]

However, as is evident in this chapter's case examples, there are many independent start-ups by Expert Idea Generators as well. Often these involve neither high technology nor extensive corporate involvement, yet they clearly reflect the expert ideas of the entrepreneur.

Five characteristics contribute to the Expert Idea Generator Pattern, and Expert Idea Generators have a majority of these qualities:

1. Desire to innovate
2. Love of ideas
3. Belief that new product development is crucial to carrying out company strategy
4. Good intelligence
5. Desire to avoid taking risks

Desire to Innovate

A desire to innovate causes Expert Idea Generators to enjoy coming up with new ideas and getting them in play. However, original or novel or creative or innovative approaches also have a distinctive quality that makes it easier to identify them as one's own, and thus take some personal credit for them. To forgo innovation is to give up the opportunity to attain a sense of self-accomplishment. A desire to introduce innovations is consistent with attaining success through one's own efforts and experiencing personal satisfaction in doing so. There is a bit of the Personal Achiever in all of this. The very fact of launching an entrepreneurial venture can be experienced as an innovative process. Those who start many businesses over time often enjoy innovation; they repeat the business founding process in order to enjoy these satisfactions again and again. For whatever reason, however, Expert Idea Generators have a strong desire to do something new.

Love of Ideas

A love of ideas involves many elements.[3] Let's look at how these elements are reflected in the Expert Idea Generator, and their effect on how tasks and problem solving are approached.

Expert Idea Generators are enthusiastic, very personal, show concern for others' views, and get along well with others. In approaching tasks they are adaptive, flexible, willing to compromise, and willing to share power. They are curious and open-minded, but want independence and dislike following rules. Those who love ideas are somewhat perfectionist and want to see many options.

Their strong motives include a desire for recognition and a desire to achieve personal goals. Such people have a high tolerance for ambiguity, prefer loose control, and may be prone to take risks.

They are intellectually tenacious, and ideological. Yet they can on occasion be somewhat unrealistic, out of touch, dogmatic about their own ideas, and not very practical. On occasion, they may be viewed as dreamers who are too idealistic and difficult to control.

Expert Idea Generators focus on long-range thinking; their time orientation is to the future. They acquire information by using intuition and discussion with others. They evaluate the information by integrating diverse cues and by applying judgment to reach conclusions. In problem solving, Expert Idea Generators keep the total problem continually in mind as the process develops. They show a tendency, willingness, and openness to continually redefine the problem. They almost simultaneously consider a variety of alternatives and options, jump around or back and forth among the elements or steps of the problem-solving process, and may at some point come to question whether the real problem has as yet even been identified. They quickly consider and discard alternatives. They may, however, be less interested in implementing solutions they develop.

People who love ideas are suffocated by stable conditions, and thus, can be extremely valuable to society because they provide a service as initiators and promoters of new enterprises, services, concepts, and ideas. When oriented more to people than to tangible things, they may be exceptionally good at diagnosing the abilities and potential of others.

Belief That New Product Development Is Crucial to Carrying Out Company Strategy

Whether or not Expert Idea Generators personally are involved in developing new products and services, they are likely to consider this approach important in a company's strategic picture. Relative to such approaches as advertising, delivery, discounts, packaging, price, quality, reciprocity, reputation, sales force, services, and variety, new product development is the major strategic factor, or it comes close. This is an index that we have found to be very important in the success of inventor-entrepreneurs and their firms.[4]

Good Intelligence

Intelligence involves capabilities such as judgment and reasoning, and the capacity to deal with abstractions, concepts, and ideas. It includes as well insightfulness, the ability to learn, and a capacity to analyze and synthesize.

When learning is required in entrepreneurship, intelligence can prove valuable. Thus Personal Achievers, Supersalespeople, and Real Managers can all benefit from good intelligence to a degree; however, other characteristics are much more important to these people. But for Expert Idea Generators, intelligence moves to the fore, simply because their activities often focus on reasoning, learning, and dealing with ideas. Intelligence can provide a leg up, a competitive advantage. It allows them to think better. Because thinking is at the center of their approach to entrepreneurship and takes up a great deal of their time, intelligence can make a big difference.

Our studies indicate, however, that intelligence at a high level, equated to what is sufficient for graduate study, is what really matters for Expert Idea Generators. The impact is most evident among scientist-entrepreneurs in high technology. The case studies in this chapter and Chapter 8 bear this out.

Desire to Avoid Taking Risks

Many people believe that taking risks is the essence of being an entrepreneur. Yet strong arguments and a good deal of research lead to a different conclusion.[5] Many entrepreneurs are extremely cautious and want to be absolutely sure before they take the plunge. This becomes crucial for Expert Idea Generators because their ideas can be quite outlandish. Furthermore, their enthusiasms can carry them away. Creative ideas have some redeeming social value; crazy ideas do not. The difference is very hard to establish when you are riding on a wave of inspirational zeal. Thus a tendency to avoid risks, to counteract the enthusiasm, to hold back and wait, to be absolutely sure the idea will work—all are essential if an Expert Idea Generator is actually to achieve success. As many of these people will tell you, creative ideas are a dime a dozen; what really matters is figuring out which ones will sell. The world of high technology, for instance, is littered with investors who were sold on an idea by a "great genius" who did not think through how the idea might be brought to market (and in fact did not care about such things).

By nature Expert Idea Generators are drawn to risks more than other entrepreneurial types. They, therefore, need an aspect of their personality that counteracts this tendency more than other entrepreneurs. Risk-taking can result in being forced out of a venture because of business failure, something they clearly want to avoid. To prevent this, Expert Idea Generators should attempt to minimize risk. A major factor in small company failure is the adoption of a strategy that places the entire company on the line, frequently in connection with some large-scale new activity (a great idea). Expert Idea Generators need to treat such ideas with skepticism.

Yet uncertainty exists in the eyes of the beholder. The ideal situation for any entrepreneur is one where others perceive that a high degree of risk exists, and thus high rewards are warranted, and the entrepreneur with his or her knowledge sees practically no risk at all.

WHAT EXPERT IDEA GENERATORS LOOK LIKE

Two case examples illustrate the Expert Idea Generator personality pattern: Patrick Whalen, who started Forwarding Services to carry out his ideas, and Patrick Welsh, who is the brains behind the turnaround of Cranz Rubber and Gasket—a corporate venture.

Patrick Whalen of Forwarding Services Inc.

Whalen thought of the idea for his company while still employed in the customer service operations of United Parcel Service. He had identified a niche that UPS was not filling and moved into it. This niche occurred because a need existed for a company to handle small packages and mail distribution for Canadian firms selling in the U.S. market. Initially Forwarding Services did warehousing for Canadian products and filled orders. Subsequently Whalen started processing mailings for Canadian firms, primarily software companies, and then put trucks on the road to bring products in from Canada. Next came a printing company to print what was mailed and a telemarketing operation to handle responses to advertisements that had been sent out. A U.S. presence for Canadian firms was created, providing prime office space in downtown Buffalo. U.S. firms have begun to use Forwarding Services to market in Canada as well.

As the firm's services expanded, it came to achieve a competitive edge simply because it could do more things than other companies. There was a synergy that others could not duplicate. Working with a customs broker, the firm developed substantial expertise in the international area. As a result of these factors, growth was rapid in the first five years of operation and the company came to achieve sales of over $3 million annually, with as many as 60 employees. In recent years recessions in the United States and a much longer-lasting one in Canada have combined to reduce sales and employment well below these figures. The loss of a very large account has also hurt. Nevertheless Forwarding Services is surviving, and its sales are now headed on up toward their former level.

Although Whalen is something of a Personal Achiever in the classic entrepreneurial pattern, his greatest strength is as an Expert Idea Generator. He loves to start new things, as the history of his business attests. Finding new niches and services is a never-ending preoccupation. He likes solving problems, which he does by considering a wide range of alternatives, remaining open to new ways of looking at things, and constantly keeping the "big picture" in mind. Routine approaches simply are not much fun. He has no difficulty in sharing power with others and has a marked tolerance for ambiguity in the world around him. Insightful, intuitive, enthusiastic, flexible, creative—all of these terms describe him. On occasion he might also be said to be idealistic, and a bit of a dreamer. He has big goals for himself.

Yet he is able to rein in these latter tendencies when the situation calls for it. In a very practical way Whalen will do anything he can to avoid taking risks. He wants to learn everything possible about a situation before he involves himself in it; he is not one to go out on thin ice. His style is one of talking over a proposed course of action with others, in order to identify any risks involved, and then taking action with full knowledge.

His Expert Idea Generator pattern is reflected as follows:

Desire to innovate	*Very High*
Love of ideas	*Very High*
Belief that new product development is crucial to carrying out company strategy	*High*
Good intelligence	*Not a factor*
Desire to avoid taking risks	*Very High*

Whalen has expanded his business (or rather businesses) into many niches. In the process he has achieved a degree of diversification that provides synergy and reduces vulnerability. He is the visionary, the one who develops and holds to strategies. It is common practice for him to work together with different partners who have specialized knowledge and skills in certain areas. He has done this with the printing and tele-marketing ends of the business. More recently, faced with a downturn in sales, he has done it with the core business. Douglas Smith, a marketing expert and Supersalesperson, has joined Forwarding Services as a co-owner with the goal of boosting sales in the fulfillment area. The results have been impressive. Whalen is always changing things and keeping the business in flux. He is constantly exploring new opportunities—operations in Mexico and in Europe for instance—but he solves real problems and does not take unnecessary risks.

Patrick Welsh of Cranz Rubber and Gasket

Welsh came to Cranz Rubber and Gasket from National Rubber, the parent company, at a time when the former was in serious financial trouble. Cranz produces gaskets and sealing devices primarily for the automotive industry, but for other industries as well. Originally it was a closely held family operation principally involved in the hose belt and die cut gasket business. A major factor in the purchase by National Rubber was that National Rubber produced closed cell sponge, which is the most significant raw material for Cranz. Welsh came to Cranz with the charge to turn it around. He has moved through positions as general manager, vice president, and ultimately president. He holds an ownership position and has considerable freedom to run the company as he sees fit.

The company markets its products in Western New York, Pennsylvania, Canada, west to Detroit, and south to Tennessee. Cranz has grown steadily from roughly a $3 million a year business to over $8 million now, in less than 10 years. Employment is up to a peak of 125, and the operation yields a solid profit. There is no question that Welsh has been able to turn the company around and make it a major contributor in the National Rubber family.

His is a managerial position in a corporate hierarchy, and it is thus not surprising that he is above average for entrepreneurs as a Real Manager. He is also somewhat above the average as a Personal Achiever. However, his major strength is in generating ideas. First and foremost Welsh is an innovator. He likes to try new approaches and to initiate new directions for a business. He is the kind of person who could easily start his own company. His major functional area early in his career was finance, but his desire to bring about change extends well beyond that specialty. He approaches problems with creativity and a broad outlook. Praise, recognition, and independence are important to him, yet these are combined with a strong commitment to his company, a willingness to share power, and considerable flexibility.

Because he is so open-minded and is always trying to find a better way, Welsh takes in a great deal of information. Such people benefit from a high level of intelligence, since they can use their intellect to process and organize their ideas. He is no exception. He is indeed very bright and he uses his capabilities very effectively. Not surprisingly he pursued an MBA degree, at Marshall University, although the press of business problems did not permit him to finish.

People like this can get caught up in their enthusiasm for ideas and take more risks than they should. Welsh is something of a risk taker outside of the work situation, but when it comes to the company's money he is much more careful. He has had more than his share of successes, and he does not want to put that record at risk by going into something of which he is not quite certain. He views new product development as a key to company growth, but not to the extent of betting on a product whose place in the market is not clearly apparent.

Welsh is unusual among Expert Idea Generators in that he is very high or high on all five of the characteristics involved.

Desire to innovate	*Very High*
Love of ideas	*High*
Belief that new product development is crucial to carrying out company strategy	*Very High*
Good intelligence	*High*
Desire to avoid taking risks	*High*

Cranz has been an ideal setting for a person of Welsh's talents. There was no place to go but up. Change has occurred everywhere. The philosophy of customer service has shifted from simple order taking to a more proactive relationship involving product quality, on-time delivery, and product engineering to preserve competitive advantage. The kinds of products have changed as Cranz moved from resale of other company's products to manufacture and to a focus on the automotive industry. There have been major technological innovations underlying changes in the methods used to produce products. Even the manufacturing location has been changed.

Basically the company markets by doing problem solving for customers or potential customers. There is no advertising. Engineering solutions are provided directly to design engineers at customer locations. This way loyalty is obtained and growth occurs. In the process new products are created to serve customers better. Yet there is a clear focus on certain core areas of technology—molded rubber solutions, acoustical and sealing foam solutions, die cutting solutions, and fabricating solutions. This has become a problem-solving company under Welsh's leadership, a company very much in tune with his own particular talents and preferences. Accordingly, the turnaround has been complete.

CONCLUSION

An Expert Idea Generator should have a majority of the following characteristics:

1. Desire to innovate
2. Love of ideas
3. Belief that new product development is crucial to carrying out company strategy
4. Good intelligence
5. Desire to avoid taking risks

Both Patrick Whalen of Forwarding Services and Patrick Welsh of Cranz Rubber and Gasket illustrate how the ideas of Expert Idea Generators often do represent very good investments, especially if they are coupled with a degree of caution that prevents taking undue risks. The desire to innovate and a love of ideas must be kept under some degree of control.

NOTES

1. This latter feature is treated extensively in a book by John J. Kao titled *Entrepreneurship, Creativity, and Organization*. If you wish to explore the field of creative endeavor further, you may want to look at *Theories of Creativity*, edited by Mark A. Runco and Robert S. Albert. This book deals with a wide range of considerations related to creative ideas.
2. These considerations are discussed in a book by Robert A. Burgelman and Leonard R. Sayles titled *Inside Corporate Innovation: Strategy, Structure, and Managerial Skills*. You should also look at an insightful volume by Edward B. Roberts called *Entrepreneurship in High Technology: Lessons from MIT and Beyond*.
3. An article by John W. Slocum and Don Hellriegel in *Business Horizons* describes the style they call "intuitive." Alan J. Rowe and Richard O. Mason in their book *Managing with Style* describe a "conceptual" style. I find these two—the intuitive and conceptual styles—to be essentially the same thing.
4. Our work on this index is described in an article in the *Journal of Business Venturing* by Norman R. Smith, Jeffrey S. Bracker, and myself.
5. On this issue you may want to look at a paper by Joel O. Raynor that is included in his book with John W. Atkinson titled *Motivation and Achievement*, as well as an article by Robert H. Brockhaus in the *Academy of Management Journal*. My own research with Norman Smith and Jeffrey Bracker leads to similar conclusions.

CHAPTER 8

How Expert Idea Generators Succeed or Fail

Chapter 7 discussed the five characteristics of Expert Idea Generators. This chapter discusses how these people follow the Idea Generating Route. What is this route, where does it start, how does it lead to success, and what traps may divert you from following it effectively?

THE IDEA GENERATING ROUTE

The Idea Generating Route involves having:

1. Sufficient knowledge to be an expert
2. The freedom to innovate and implement ideas
3. Skills, or access to skills, that complement those of the Expert Idea Generator

Expert Idea Generators are distinguished from other types of entrepreneurs by being experts at something. Thus, there is a period during which they become experts, followed by an opportunity to think of ways to put this expertise to work in novel and creative ways. Often Expert Idea Generators are able to take their thinking to the frontiers of knowledge in an area, and then because they know enough to understand where the frontiers are located, they can go one step beyond. This one step has the potential for giving a sizable competitive advantage, simply because no one else is operating there.[1]

Thus, the Idea Generating Route must contain a period in which people are educated up to the point of being an expert. The case examples later in this chapter describe some of the ways this may occur. However, to the extent possible, formal education appears to offer sizable advantages over learning on the job. The emphasis in formal education is entirely on learning, and material is presented with the learning objective clearly in mind. More informal learning on the job may be less economical simply because it is interspersed with a great deal of "doing," and perhaps some irrelevant learning in addition. On the other hand many important aspects of business are not taught in school. Certain whole fields of business activity simply are not to be found within formal education. Expert Idea Generators can succeed in many areas without much formal education at all, simply because formal education does not deal extensively with the ideas that concern them. The key: Determine what knowledge is needed and whether it can best be gained on the job, in school, or through some combination of these.

Because of the time needed for learning, Expert Idea Generators tend to be somewhat older than other entrepreneurs when they start their ventures. They also dislike, and shy away from, highly structured and regulated employment situations. They need the freedom to think for themselves, to have ideas, even if not very good ones that they later discard. This freedom to create and try out ideas is crucial to the Idea Generating Route. Often what pushes Expert Idea Generators into entrepreneurship is feeling stifled where they are.

Entrepreneurship can offer that freedom. However, if Expert Idea Generators can find the same freedom elsewhere, they may never need to become entrepreneurs. Many academic settings, research laboratories, professional firms, and the like offer this freedom. As with Supersalespeople and Real Managers, Expert Idea Generators may have successful careers outside entrepreneurship—as research scientists, writers, corporate planners, and the like. Many, however, do find success as entrepreneurs. A big factor in the entrepreneurial decision for people with the Expert Idea Generator pattern is whether they already have a work situation that permits use of their talents. Not infrequently what appears to be a very positive work setting begins to go bad for some reason, and becomes more restrictive. At that point the transition to entrepreneurship becomes almost automatic. It is the only apparent way to follow the Idea Generating trajectory.

Some Expert Idea Generators work better with certain partners, often partners that add other psychological patterns or areas of expertise to the business. As the firm grows, the need for managerial skills becomes important exactly as it does for Personal Achievers. Expert Idea Generators can "hit the wall" too.

Expert Idea Generators benefit from also being a Personal Achiever,

Supersalesperson, or Real Manager. Following the Idea Generating Route appears to be more successful when other capabilities are brought to bear. However, those whose entrepreneurial talents are limited to the Expert Idea Generator pattern only can still follow the Idea Generating Route to success by focusing on the visionary role in the firm. Many also appear to benefit from some type of backing by a parent corporation, a relative, an "angel," or anyone else who can provide resources while imposing relatively few restrictions on the entrepreneur's freedom. Backing of this kind may in fact be essential to carrying out the Expert Idea Generator's ideas. (In talking to Expert Idea Generators I heard about a number of benevolent benefactors.)

The case example of Hal Leader that follows illustrates many of the ways in which the characteristics of the Expert Idea Generator mesh with the Idea Generating Route. If Leader had not been an Expert Idea Generator it is unlikely his firm would have survived in a rapidly changing industry in which companies were failing all around him.

Harold Leader of Printing Prep Inc.

Printing Prep was founded as a typesetting operation by Harold Leader, who got into the area first by selling business cards in high school, then via a college degree in printing management from Rochester Institute of Technology, and subsequently through experience with a major printing firm. He left the latter to establish his own company because he could not convince his employers to purchase the new IBM Composer, which had just come on the market and which represented in his view a major technological advance. Printing Prep was an opportunity to take over a market niche at the expense of his former employer, who did not appear to be aggressively pursuing that niche.

The company typesets headlines, forms, price lists, directories, annual reports, newsletters, magazines, brochures, and the like for printers, advertising agencies, in-house company printing operations, freelance artists, and others. It does typesetting, mechanicals, stats for advertisements, headline type, color packaging mockups, and color copies. Recently it has moved into the desktop publishing field, helping customers use this technology more effectively.

Under Leader, Printing Prep grew steadily over a 20-year period; it did $2 million annually in sales and employed 50 people before recession hit. It was quite profitable because it was able to charge prices above the industry average for a quality product and excellent service. During the recession the firm lost ground, as did most of the printing industry, but unlike many other companies it stayed in business. More recently Printing Prep has been able to improve its position to a point where it is now essentially back to the level existing before the recession. Over time it has been a highly successful company in an industry that has experienced major technological change and many business failures.

Leader is above average among entrepreneurs as a Personal Achiever, but his major strength is in the area of Expert Idea Generator. He is a real innovator who loves to find new ways to do things and new services to provide to the marketplace. In this way he places his own unique imprint on what he does. His company very much reflects his own ideas. Challenges fascinate him to the point where he really does not enjoy situations that remain stable over long periods. He is original, imaginative, even creative in his work. He looks at problems in all their aspects, considering many alternatives and their future consequences. He is very adaptive and flexible, and may seem a bit disorganized to others of a less idea-oriented bent, but there is clear method in his madness. Learning about new approaches is fun for him and his commitment to the printing profession is intense.

The risk with people like this is that in following their intuition wherever it takes them, they may bet too much on what turns out to be "a crazy idea" and suffer major losses, if not total failure. Leader has no such problem. A strong tendency to avoid risks keeps him from overextending himself. He does his homework and is capable of rejecting ideas that, although they engage his enthusiasm, do not appear fully viable or are too costly. Gambling on long shots has no appeal; he wants a sure thing where his special knowledge gives him a competitive advantage.

His personality pattern closely matches the Expert Idea Generator model.

Desire to innovate	*Very High*
Love of ideas	*Very High*
Belief that new product development is crucial to carrying out company strategy	*High*
Good intelligence	*Not a Factor*
Desire to avoid taking risks	*Very High*

Printing is a capital-intensive business with equipment obsolescence coming very quickly. New technology is always on the horizon. The trick is to balance costs and opportunities to make decisions that will yield the best results. Leader is a master of this process. He scans the environment constantly, reading trade journals and going to trade shows. He learns everything he can about new equipment and the possible uses to which it may be put. He is constantly exploring new market opportunities—the retailing of color copying, mail order approaches, and the laser printing of signs, among others. He probes these niches, investing as little as possible until he learns enough to be sure of where he is going. The move into desktop publishing occurred as a well-researched defensive effort to avoid being upstaged by a new technology.

Printing Prep survived in the early years because it had a technological edge with the IBM Composer. It has maintained this edge by constantly reinvesting in new equipment. New ideas are the lifeblood of the business. As computers evolved, the company has gotten into telecommunications, mainframe computers, disk conversions, scanning devices, and much more. Almost all of these technological and market innovations have been the brainchild of Harold Leader. His role throughout has been to keep his company in the forefront of advances in the field.

GETTING STARTED ON THE IDEA GENERATING ROUTE

Of the 100 established entrepreneurs in Western New York that I studied, 33 were Expert Idea Generators. Table 7 shows that start-ups occur about as often among the Expert Idea Generators as with the other three entrepreneurial types. There is a difference, however. Expert Idea Generators are much more likely to start firms without partners (34 percent) than with them (15 percent).

Expert Idea Generators favor independent start-ups because they are then free to develop their own ideas. Harold Leader is an example of this. Partners can complement the talents of Expert Idea Generators and provide assistance in developing ideas, as in the Chapter 7 case of Patrick Whalen of Forwarding Services. But more often than not Expert Idea Generators see partners as a potential limitation; the partner may not be as enthusiastic about the ideas of the Expert Idea Generator and may try to take the company in a different direction. Also, because Expert Idea Generators are unilaterally focused on their own ideas and a firm that will put them into action, they may not attract partners very easily.

The other information in Table 7 is similar to that contained in previous tables for the other three entrepreneurial types with one major excep-

Table 7   HOW EXPERT IDEA GENERATORS
BECOME ENTREPRENEURS

Started Firm Without Partners	34%
Started Firm With Partners	15
Purchased Firm	12
Took Over Family Firm	18
Initiated Corporate Venture	0
Was Turnaround Person in Corporate Venture	18
Started Sales or Professional Practice	3
Total	100%

tion: although Expert Idea Generators do not initiate corporate ventures, they certainly do work to turn them around (18 percent). This is primarily because they have ideas that are recognized as offering a potential solution to the existing problems. This certainly was the case for Patrick Welsh at Cranz Rubber and Gasket. If existing ventures or subsidiaries or components of businesses are in trouble and need to be revived, hiring an Expert Idea Generator and giving that person the freedom to put his or her ideas to work is a strategy well worth pursuing. Providing an ownership share to go with the freedom is important also.

SUCCESS ON THE
IDEA GENERATING ROUTE

Table 8 demonstrates that the Idea Generating Route can lead to a sizable degree of success: 37 percent of Expert Idea Generator firms were in the "Firm Has Grown a Lot" category. That contrasts to 0 percent for the 27 individuals in the group of 100 who did not have a strong entrepreneurial pattern in any of the four areas.

Table 8 also shows that being hurt by recession is not frequent, although it can occur, as the case of Hal Leader of Printing Prep demonstrates; it is more likely when the entrepreneur is an Expert Idea Generator only.

Expert Idea Generators who are separated from their original firm are most likely to start a new venture; the desire for freedom to follow the Idea Generating Route does not disappear simply because a particular venture did not work out. Consequently, Expert Idea Generators are likely to get back into entrepreneuring as quickly as possible, in order to take another shot at putting their vision into practice.

Table 8   HOW EXPERT IDEA
GENERATOR'S FIRMS SUCCEEDED

Entrepreneur and Firm Stayed Together	
Firm Has Grown a Lot	37%
Firm Has Grown Some	24
Recession Has Hurt Firm	6
Firm Has Only Survived	3
Entrepreneur and Firm No Longer Together	
Left Firm and Started New Venture	9
Left Firm and Had Nonentrepreneurial Career Subsequently	3
Insufficient Information Available	18
Total	100%

Expert Idea Generators are experts. To succeed on the Idea Generating Route they must have a very good education, if their business is in an area where formal education teaches the needed knowledge. The case of Gerald Murak shows how this education can contribute to following the Idea Generating Route. On the other hand if formal education has relatively little to offer, education through experience is crucial. Timothy Thill grew up in the chocolate business in Western New York, an area that has a heavy concentration of firms in that industry. The examples that follow—Murak and Thill—show how different people with different beginnings may follow the Idea Generating Route to success.

Gerald Murak of J. C. Brock, Gerald Murak & Associates, and Chameleon Color Cards Ltd.

J. C. Brock Corporation is an Employee Stock Ownership Plan (E.S.O.P.) company, although control still resides in the founding family. It provides fresh produce to retail customers and food service distributors in the Northeast and parts of Canada. Products are purchased from growers and packers, inspected, prepared, and packaged under the Brock label, as well as under various private labels. The company has grown to over $20 million in sales per year and to over 200 employees.

Murak was hired from General Mills to serve as operations manager with responsibility for safety, quality, sanitation, production, engineering, maintenance, scheduling, and transportation. The E.S.O.P. arrangement had shifted power down into the hands of the employees, at least to some extent, and the company wished to consolidate this process. Murak was thus brought in as a change agent. His background was in industrial education, and he held a master's degree from Buffalo State College in that area. He had considerable training and experience in areas such as total quality management, team building, and employee empowerment.

Consistent with his position at both General Mills and J. C. Brock, he is indeed a Real Manager. But to an even greater extent, and this is where being a change agent comes in, he is an Expert Idea Generator. He enjoys thinking up ways of making improvements in a situation and carrying these ideas out. He is adept at diagnosing the abilities and potential of others and in figuring out ways to motivate them. He is insightful, shows concern for others' views, is rather independent, and utilizes an open and participative leadership style that brings out the best in those who work for him. Developing new products and services is important in his scheme of things. He believes in shared decision making and he wants to operate in contexts where this is possible. Yet he is able to constrain his enthusiasm for new ideas if they lack practical relevance, and he will not empower subordinates to do things if they lack the knowledge to do them effectively.

On the tests measuring the Expert Idea Generator type, Murak looks as follows:

Desire to innovate	*High*
Love of ideas	*Very High*
Belief that new product development is crucial to carrying out company strategy	*High*
Good intelligence	*Not a Factor*
Desire to avoid taking risks	*High*

At J. C. Brock, Murak made many changes quite rapidly. Company-wide meetings were introduced, employee surveys were conducted, a team-based bonus plan was implemented, the organization structure was flattened, quality assurance was strengthened, systems improvement teams were put in place, long-range planning meetings were held, employees were empowered in the budget process, safety programs were created, jobs were combined, and much more. These changes had some very positive results for productivity, injury rates, employee morale, and efficiency. However, certain succession issues could not be resolved, and before long there was a parting of the ways.

At this point Murak decided to establish Gerald Edward Murak & Associates to make his change agent skills more widely available, something he had considered for a long time. The firm was founded "to share proven continuous improvement techniques which focus on quality and performance by optimizing human potential." In this role he has served as facilitator for the quality improvement process of a rapidly growing service company, developed a shared mission statement for a corporation, and generated from the company team over 200 ideas to improve their bottom line, created a total quality training program for a nonprofit organization, and so on. He is very busy. Among other things he lectures and conducts training on such topics as total quality, setup reduction, statistical tracking, return on people investments, team leadership, creative problem solving, and crosstraining. His consulting firm is really the actualization of what he is.

More recently Murak has added another activity to this portfolio, starting up the U.S. operations of Chameleon Color Cards, a division of an established Canadian firm doing business globally, which helps corporations to market color. The company has grown to some 50 employees, and he is actively implementing his ideas regarding self-directed teams with these people, while continuing to serve other clients through Gerald Edward Murak & Associates. Very recently he has begun to provide interim management to a second corporation in addition to his work with Chameleon, again emphasizing self-directed teams and his ideas regarding employee empowerment. He has also started work on an MBA degree at the State University of New York at Buffalo to further augment his expertise.

Timothy Thill of Choco-Logo and Tomric Plastics

Tomric Plastics is a family business now owned entirely by Timothy Thill. It manufactures thermo-formed plastic molds for the confectionery industry. The company has some 2,000 different stock molds available and also makes customized plastic molds. Choco-Logo was until recently a division of Tomric Plastics. It is a custom chocolate manufacturer serving hotels, corporations, and retail outlets by providing products for advertising, promotions, gift giving, and resale. Choco-Logo was started by Thomas Elsinghorst, Thill's stepbrother, then merged into Tomric, and has recently been sold off. Thill, though still young, headed Choco-Logo and now heads Tomric.

At the present time Tomric does something more than $1 million in sales annually and has 20 employees. It has always been a profitable business and is now in the process of moving toward becoming a high-volume producer in its industry.

Although Thill is about equally high as both a Real Manager and an Expert Idea Generator, the latter characteristic will be given particular attention here. However, it is important to note that this combination of factors has operated to produce a special concern for both social causes and economic performance. Thill is clearly idealistic and ideological in his approach, but his managerial orientation keeps him from being unrealistic and impractical. He is creative, has a broad outlook, and is concerned about the future. As a manager he is adaptive and flexible, shows concern for the views of others, and is somewhat prone to take risks. He likes to change things and is dedicated to making the world a better place to live. The day-to-day problems of his business are of concern to him and he enjoys tackling them with imagination and enthusiasm, but he is the kind of person who also reaches out and finds problems in the world around him; these too provide subject matter for his fertile mind and probing intuition. He values praise and wants recognition, but at the same time he is willing to put a great deal of thought and effort into activities that will yield them. Given his predilection for creative innovation, it is not surprising that he puts new product development at the head of his list of the company's strategies.

Thill's personality profile as an Expert Idea Generator is particularly strong with respect to his love of ideas.

Desire to innovate	*High*
Love of ideas	*Very High*
Belief that new product development is crucial *to carrying out company strategy*	*Very High*
Good intelligence	*Not a Factor*
Desire to avoid taking risks	*Not a Factor*

Consistent with his idealism, Thill has been deeply involved with ideas related to helping the homeless and hungry throughout the world. As part of a program for health through housing, he has participated in community development planning for the homeless in Honduras. There have been other social causes as well. After Choco-Logo was sold, he spent a year in the formerly communist countries of Eastern Europe attempting to develop business relationships and broker deals. These efforts have produced some business, and Thill continues to work on them.

As president of Tomric Plastics, he has been making a number of changes and expediting others that were initiated previously. The company has moved strongly into serving supermarket chains with the intent of becoming a higher-volume producer. New equipment has been introduced as well as new methods of production. As a result, there has been an expansion in the types of products that could be manufactured. Tomric has entered into plastic packaging on a more extensive scale than before. Plans are in process to expand locations beyond the present plant. Perhaps most important, Thill has helped to introduce into the company a culture that emphasizes growth and new ideas. He wants very much to put his own imprint on the business.

The knowledge base for all these changes does not come from Thill's formal education. He has completed only a few college courses, and none are particularly relevant to his business. He has, however, worked in that business since he was a young boy, and he was literally brought up in the chocolate industry.

AVOIDING THE TRAPS ALONG THE IDEA GENERATING ROUTE

I find four types of problems that can make it difficult for an Expert Idea Generator to follow the Idea Generating Route closely.

The Ideas of the Expert Idea Generator Are Stifled

Expert Idea Generators can be diverted from the Idea Generating Route when their ideas are stifled by a work environment that does the following:

- Stresses that there is only one best way of doing things
- Reacts quickly and negatively to any expression of new ideas
- Opposes anything that is not easy to understand
- Emphasizes that new ideas bring only trouble
- Sees that rewards never go to people who produce new ideas
- Keeps people with new ideas under tight control and, if that does not work, ostracizes them

Expert Idea Generators escape to entrepreneurship to gain freedom from these kinds of work environments. However, an escape to entrepreneuring can be doomed, also. Corporate ventures, family businesses, situations where equity is lost to investors and venture capitalists—all of these can produce environments just as negative for ideas as the one described above. Even a solely owned start-up can stifle ideas if there are not resources to carry out the ideas. This is why benevolent benefactors can be so important to the success of Expert Idea Generators. Without question the most important single factor contributing to a separation of the Expert Idea Generator from the Idea Generating Route is the existence of such an inhibiting environment. It is almost impossible to create and develop ideas in these situations.

The antidote: Get rid of this environment. If you cannot change it, leave it. Ideas are the talent and advantage you can bring to being an entrepreneur. If an environment strips you of this, it leaves you with very little to offer, and no chance of success. Often Expert Idea Generators become involved in lengthy struggles against the idea-stifling forces, usually to no avail. The conflict takes all of their energies, and the venture suffers.

And, if the likelihood of changing your environment is low, at least start planning your strategic retreat from this hostile environment. Expert Idea Generators, like Patrick Whalen and Gerald Murak, seem to be able to land on their feet again and again.

The Expert Idea Generator Never Becomes an Expert

Sometimes Expert Idea Generators do not become full-fledged experts; the ideas that they generate are so-to-speak "half baked." This can happen in a number of ways—not taking enough time to become expert, poor education, learning on the job that does not expose you to the really important information, and so on.

Learning within a family business can be particularly risky in this regard. If the business has gotten behind in some way, and the learning that is needed does not exist there, you can learn by rising within the family business as Tim Thill did and never become a full-scale expert. Thill avoided this, but you may not. The problem: You may think you have reached expert knowledge because you have never been exposed to anything else beyond what the family business has to offer, and that is not enough.

The antidote: Take the time to be sure that you really are an expert capable of developing really sound ideas. Remember that successful Expert Idea Generators tend to be older when they start their ventures. There is a good reason for that—learning takes time. If you have most of your experience in a family business, try a stint in another business in the same industry. If you have most of your formal education at one school, try another or start reading widely in your field.

The Expert Idea Generator Wanders
Off the Idea Generating Route

It is also possible for an Expert Idea Generator to get diverted from the Idea Generating Route on an entirely voluntary basis. Some entrepreneurs become expert in one area and then think they see an opportunity in another area, thus leaving their area of expertise. For example if a banker, with small business loan experience, who is really a financial expert, purchases a business in some other area such as manufacturing, the ideas of a financial nature simply will not be sufficient in the new area.

Similarly, it is important that as an Expert Idea Generator you remain in the visionary role, developing ideas in which you believe. If you are drawn heavily into general management or sales, especially if your idea is not involved, you can get diverted from the Idea Generating Route, and trouble is to be expected.

The antidote: Be sure you know what you are expert at, and stick with it. Hire someone to do the things you should not be doing. In the first instance, it is important to be honest with yourself. Nobody is an expert at everything. If you are having difficulty putting boundaries around your area of expertise, talk to established experts and see what they have to say.

Often Expert Idea Generators need to hire general managers to avoid hitting the wall as a business grows. I know of one entrepreneur who went outside and hired an experienced manager whom he installed as president of the company. The entrepreneur took the title Senior Scientist. These solutions make a lot of sense.

Success Strips Off the Risk Avoidance That Permitted It

Over time there is a risk that firms started by Expert Idea Generators will retire into themselves. Ideas and invention become not only the name of the game but the only game; they serve as an end in themselves, while client needs are ignored. In this scenario the company's strategy becomes one of technological or ideological escapism, its goal a kind of technical utopia. The culture moves to that of a think tank, rather than a competitive firm, and the structure of the organization disintegrates into chaos.[2] What is described here is a company that mirrors the innovation of the Expert Idea Generator, but lacks the pragmatism that comes with a desire to avoid risks. It is as if success has stripped off the risk avoidance feature. This can begin to happen at any time when success has accumulated to the point where the entrepreneur is no longer concerned about failure. In my experience, it does not necessarily take more than a few years to reach that point, if the early ideas were very good and made for rapid growth.

The antidote: If you are an Expert Idea Generator, you are always capable of having really terrible ideas. Never forget that. Never let the megalomania of success lead you to forgo the pragmatism of your desire to avoid risks. Risk avoidance got you there, and it will keep you there. Expert Idea Generators cannot afford to be without it.

CONCLUSION

As with Supersalespeople and Real Managers, Expert Idea Generators can have very successful careers without ever entering the world of entrepreneurship. Typically they enter that world because they see it as providing an opportunity to create and develop ideas, an opportunity that is lacking elsewhere. In working with and counseling these people, I find it necessary to evaluate the whole context of the decision to enter into a venture. Similarly those who are making such a decision need to look at the whole range of career alternatives available to them. Entrepreneurship is only one way to actuate the talents of an Expert Idea Generator, although it is a very important and appropriate one. In any event it is crucial that if you choose to be an entrepreneur you follow the Idea Generating Route.

This route involves:

- Becoming an expert in a specific field
- Having the freedom to use that expert knowledge to innovate
- Having skills, or access to skills, that complement those of the Expert Idea Generator

There are traps on that route that can divert Expert Idea Generators, or even prevent them from entering it at all:

1. Their ideas are stifled by people or circumstances beyond their control.
2. They fail to learn enough to become the expert that following the Idea Generating Route requires.
3. They wander into areas where their expertise is no longer sufficient to yield a competitive edge.
4. They achieve so much success and become so confident of their ideas that they no longer apply risk avoidance to their thinking.

The case examples in this chapter and Chapter 7 show how Expert Idea Generators operate outside the high technology area, because Western New York is not a hotbed of high technology like Route 128 around Boston and Silicon Valley in California. High technology, however, is much more in the news these days.[3] Yet I believe the examples I have included are more typical for the country as a whole.

The forte of Expert Idea Generators is innovation and ideas. These can be used in a wide range of industries and circumstances, of which high technology is only one. What is important is that you find an environment conducive to your ideas.

NOTES

1. This formulation draws on a book by Calvin W. Taylor titled *Climate for Creativity* and on a more recent statement by Michael B. McCaskey in his book *The Executive Challenge.*
2. This is the picture Danny Miller presents in *The Icarus Paradox.* He is talking about very large firms of this kind that have gone into decline, but I believe the problem is more widespread than that.
3. The best source of information and examples of these high technology entrepreneurs is a book by Edward B. Roberts titled *Entrepreneurs in High Technology.*

CHAPTER 9

When More Than One Pattern Is Prominent: The Complex Entrepreneur

Possessing multiple entrepreneurial patterns, and thus having the potential to follow more than one route, gives a major advantage to an entrepreneur. People with two strong patterns have an advantage over those with only one. People with three strong patterns have an even greater advantage. And those with four strong patterns have a singular competitive advantage. I call these people with multiple patterns complex entrepreneurs. They can bring a range of skills to bear, depending on the particular needs of the enterprise.

This chapter will give you an understanding of what a complex entrepreneur looks like, how their talents may be used in a venture, and how complex entrepreneurs of different types achieve success.

Although the case examples in earlier chapters were selected to provide a picture of one type of strong pattern at a time, a number of these people are in fact complex entrepreneurs.

Both Jacqueline Taylor of Stovroff and Taylor Travel and Richard Pohlman of Pohlman Foundry Company (Chapter 1), in addition to being Personal Achievers, are Supersalespeople.

In Chapter 2 Darwin Dennison of DINE Systems and Harold Hibbard of United Building Services are indeed strong Personal Achievers, but Dennison is also an Expert Idea Generator and Hibbard a Supersalesperson.

Two of the examples discussed in Chapter 6 are also complex entrepreneurs. Daniel Blatz of Supplemental Health Care Services is not only a Real Manager, but a Personal Achiever as well. The same two patterns are present in Gary Posluszny of K.D.M. Die Company.

Finally, in Chapter 8, Gerald Murak of J. C. Brock (as well as Gerald Murak & Associates and Chameleon Color Cards Ltd.) and Timothy Thill of Choco-Logo and Tomric Plastics both are not only Expert Idea Generators but Real Managers also.

As you gain an understanding of complex entrepreneurs and how they use their talents to attain success, looking back at these eight cases may help to give you additional insight.

HOW FREQUENT ARE COMPLEX ENTREPRENEURS

In my group of 100 established entrepreneurs from Western New York, 38 percent are complex entrepreneurs—essentially the same percentage as exists within the case examples presented in earlier chapters. The 38 percent is made up of 27 percent who have two strong patterns, 10 percent with three strong patterns and only 1 percent—one person—with all four patterns. Not only does adding to the number of patterns make for a greater likelihood of success, it becomes increasingly rare.

Also, understand that these figures are for established entrepreneurs who have weathered many of the storms that go with venture start-ups—and survived. In less selected groups complex entrepreneurs are found less frequently. For example, among MBA students in entrepreneurship courses at the State University of New York at Buffalo, complexity occurs less than half as often as in the 100 established entrepreneur group, and only 3 percent have three or more strong patterns. On balance the special talents of a complex entrepreneur are unlikely to exist widely in the general population.

Although any combination of patterns may be present in a particular complex entrepreneur, certain combinations are more frequent than others. When there are two strong patterns, the Personal Achiever and Real Manager combination occurs most often. Next most frequent is the Real Manager combined with the Expert Idea Generator. When there are three strong patterns, the most likely combination is Personal Achiever, Real Manager, and Expert Idea Generator. These combinations are very effective types of complexity because they permit a shift to the Managing Route as the firm grows.

Are certain patterns particularly likely to bond with at least one additional pattern, and are other patterns more likely to stand alone? Based on the 100 established entrepreneurs, consider the following:

Personal Achievers have another strong pattern 86 percent of the time, and are only Personal Achievers 14 percent of the time.
Supersalespeople have another strong pattern 48 percent of the time, and are only Supersalespeople 52 percent of the time.

Real Managers have another strong pattern 82 percent of the time, and are only Real Managers 18 percent of the time.

Expert Idea Generators have another strong pattern 67 percent of the time, and are only Expert Idea Generators 33 percent of the time.

Clearly with a Supersalesperson, there is a lower probability of having another strong pattern. In particular being a Supersalesperson does not go with being a Personal Achiever. With so many Supersalespeople lacking an alternative to following the Selling Route, the need these people have for judicious staffing of other activities within the firm becomes even more apparent.

Another important point: the great majority of Personal Achievers, and Real Managers too, have another strong pattern. Mostly these two patterns are found together. But even if they are not, the propensity Personal Achievers and Real Managers have for complexity represents a major added source of entrepreneurial strength.

SEQUENTIAL AND CONCOMITANT USE OF MULTIPLE PATTERNS

Having multiple patterns means that an entrepreneur personally can, if necessary, range across a larger number of activities when the firm is at various stages in its growth. They can control more and need to delegate less. When multiple patterns exist, they may be used in a sequential manner; for example when a firm grows and a Personal Achiever hits the wall, the Real Manager pattern is activated. Multiple patterns may also be put to use concomitantly; a Supersalesperson who is also an Expert Idea Generator devotes his or her energies to selling, and also to creating ideas and being a visionary—thus following the Selling and Expert Idea Generating Routes at the same time.

Let me take up the sequential and concomitant approaches in more detail using case examples. Leon Smith of Niagara Lubricant Company, our only four-pattern entrepreneur, provides an example of the sequencing pattern. The case of Russell Fenton of Fenton, Weber, & Jones Packaging illustrates the concomitant use of patterns.

Leon Smith of Niagara Lubricant Company

Niagara Lubricant was founded by Smith's grandfather and subsequently run by his grandmother and later his father before he took over. It is a compounder and blender of lubricants as well as a distributor of major brands. Products include metalworking fluids, greases, gear oil, hydraulic oil, rust preventatives, recycled industrial oils, and the like. At times in the past the company has been a distributorship only, but it is now heavily involved in manufacturing; it sells to industrial users of its products.

Both sales and profits have been up and down over the years, although there were long periods when business was very good indeed. In the period before Smith took over from his father, however, the company was not doing well, and it was almost sold. In fact only Smith's last-minute decision to try to keep the company afloat rescued it from being bought out by a competitor. At this time it was not profitable and had run up substantial debt. Problems included a lack of financial controls, poor inventory controls, no marketing strategy, incorrect information from the computer system, the wrong product and market emphasis, and generally laissez-faire management. In recent years many of these factors have been corrected, and Niagara Lubricant has returned to profitability. Its sales are now up to $5.5 million a year, and there are 28 employees.

Smith is one of those rare entrepreneurs whose profile exhibits high scores in all four areas. He is best characterized as a Real Manager, but he is only slightly less a Personal Achiever and again slightly less still an Expert Idea Generator. He is a Supersalesperson as well, but this factor is not quite as strong. As a Real Manager he exhibits a strong emphasis on efficiency and the use of controls, is highly competitive (he was a championship golfer at one time), and finds it easy to organize the work of others. Decisions present no problem for him, and he is secure in himself. There is no question that he runs his company.

As a Personal Achiever Smith's achievement drive is manifested in considerable pride in what he is able to accomplish. He likes to plan, and he believes planning is worthwhile because he, not others or mere chance, determines his own destiny. He brings a tremendous amount of energy to everything he does, and that produces a good deal of tension. He wants to make the key decisions regarding what he does at work, utilizing his own goals and plans as a guide. It is easy for him to become totally immersed in his company and its needs.

He loves to do things differently and introduce changes. In this sense he is a classic Expert Idea Generator. Figuring out new ways to solve problems, new marketing strategies and niches, new products to introduce—these are the things he enjoys most about his position. Although he did not finish college, he is very bright and this gives him an advantage in thinking up ways to outsmart the competition.

Smith tends to manage a sale in many instances, but as a Supersalesperson there is also a softer side to his approach. He really wants to help people and this comes through in his dealings with customers. He also tends to find the best in others; being hypercritical is not at all his way. Sales and marketing strategy is something he understands and he views it as the most important factor in his company's success. For a number of years he was in fact the number one salesman at Niagara Lubricant. That was before he put on another hat, became a full-time manager, and ultimately president of the company.

It is apparent that Smith is a complex person, and that complexity is clearly evident in the things he has done to turn his company around and move it forward. For a time the company was in automotive and coolant applications; that has shifted to the industrial market. Manufacturing has been reemphasized with the move into a new facility and the purchase of another manufacturing company. Major technological advances in chemical engineering have changed the way products are made and several new products have been introduced. A machine that takes used oils and other petroleum-based fluids and recycles them back to their original quality is now on stream. This is part of the company's planned move in the environmental area.

A human resource consultant has been brought in to assist with staffing. A number of new people have been hired as a result, the objective being to create a managerial team that would compensate for Smith's own weaknesses on the financial and technical sides. Salespeople have been added as well and the sales compensation program has been redesigned. There is more training as well.

A variety of management systems have been introduced to give Smith a better handle on what is happening in the company. Financial controls are now in place, the computer system has been improved, and inventory is moving out more quickly. Change is everywhere and it is being managed efficiently. This requires a great deal of time and effort, but for a person like Smith that is no problem at all. Above all there is a plan in place and the company is now being managed so as to make that plan a reality.

For a considerable period of time Smith was a Supersalesperson following the Selling Route. His other patterns were largely left dormant in this period. With increasing sales, and particularly after he took charge, the company began to grow. His role as a visionary expanded and his skills as an Expert Idea Generator became engaged. At first, as a business owner, Smith operated largely as a Personal Achiever getting his ideas in motion, but even then his family business was large enough to utilize his skills as a Real Manager to some extent. Gradually he appears to be following the Managing Route more and the Selling Route less; now he manages the sales process, rather than being the top salesperson, and he manages most other aspects of the business as well. Sequencing has meant that the Personal Achiever and Supersalesperson patterns, which dominated in the early years, have been largely replaced by the Expert Idea Generator and Real Manager patterns.

Russell Fenton of Fenton, Weber, & Jones Packaging

Russell Fenton and John Jones own Fenton, Weber, & Jones Packaging. They started the company together, with Jones as president and Fenton as vice president of sales and marketing. A third partner was bought out at an early point. Basically the company is a sales and distribution operation; it purchases its products from vendors. These products are all types of rigid plastic packaging, such as bottles and other containers, which are used by industries such as cosmetics, pharmaceuticals, and the like. In addition to distribution of products to the filling location, the company provides consultation on packaging matters and engineering services. It has strong niches in bristling, roll-on dispensing systems, as well as custom-molded components. It markets throughout the United States and in Canada.

Company sales have expanded at a rate of roughly $1 million a year to the current level of over $10 million. There are 17 employees. Although the industry is very competitive and relatively easy to enter, the company has remained profitable throughout the 10 years of its existence.

Fenton grew up in a military family and graduated from Bowling Green State University, where he majored in marketing and held a wide range of campus leadership positions. After college he started in sales with Owens-Illinois and then moved on and up with Empire State Bottle Company, where he and Jones worked together. Thus he had almost 10 years of corporate experience before the company start-up occurred.

As a complex entrepreneur Fenton has two major strengths. One is that he is a Personal Achiever; this fits the stereotype of the classic entrepreneur, and the route he has followed as well. Second, he is a Real Manager. The latter pattern manifests itself in a strong desire to take charge of a situation in the interest of efficiency and results. Power and authority are important factors in the mix of personal motivation for such people. They like to lead. Managers must tell others what to do when necessary and back up their statements with appropriate actions. Fenton does this in dealing with subordinates and uses much the same style in managing sales to customers. He enjoys having subordinates to manage and customers to sell to. His approach in the latter instances would usually be characterized as a hard sell, but nonetheless it is very effective. In particular he likes to stand out by making presentations to groups of customers, a procedure he performs very well.

Fenton has a real talent in dealing with his employees on a face-to-face basis. He exhibits a great deal of self-confidence, which reflects on his presentation of his company's capabilities. He is decisive and knows what he wants. He understands what his talents are and wants to use these strengths to the fullest. There is no sense in which he is insecure. All of these factors contribute to an affinity for leadership roles that has characterized him throughout his life.

As a Personal Achiever Fenton has a very strong desire to achieve success. He drives hard and gets great satisfaction from any evidence that his firm is growing and increasing its market share. Planning and setting goals for future accomplishment are things he likes to do. He is constantly looking for opportunities, initiating courses of action for his company. Believing that what he does can make a big difference, his style is to push forward and get things moving whenever the situation seems to warrant it. Like most Personal Achievers, he is an individualist who likes his freedom and enjoys the satisfaction that comes with his accomplishments. And these accomplishments are indeed quite considerable, commensurate with the huge amount of energy he invests in his work.

Fenton is responsible for customer service, sales, and marketing, while his partner Jones handles accounting, technical services, and purchasing. This appears to be a good matchup. Both share the vision, planning, and growth strategies of the firm. Fenton is taking steps to expand the sales force, introduce a more effective sales compensation program, establish a sales training program, and refine the marketing effort. Major strategies are being implemented to introduce more creative product designs and to achieve a higher-quality input from vendors. Fenton is a good crisis manager. The company has been very effective in obtaining publicity in industry publications. In short, this is a well-managed marketing effort.

In addition, Fenton is constantly on the road selling to major accounts himself. And he wants to grow the company as well, perhaps to give him more to manage. Moving into manufacturing is always a possibility. Acquisitions are frequently explored. Fenton and Jones between them make for a vibrant and dynamic organization.

Over the life of the firm Fenton has followed the Achieving Route, consistent with the relatively small number of employees. He has devoted his Real Manager talents to external selling primarily, although there is certainly evidence of his managing internally as well. All this has gone on hand in glove, moving frequently back and forth across routes. What could be a tendency to overmanage in a firm this small is buffered by his Personal Achiever pattern, his partner, and the fact that he devotes many of his Real Manager talents to direct selling. To date the two strong patterns have been used concomitantly. Yet Fenton definitely wants to grow the firm to a size where his Real Manager skills can be put to use more fully within the firm. Thus sequencing may be his approach of the future.

GETTING STARTED WHEN YOU HAVE THE TALENT TO FOLLOW MULTIPLE ROUTES

As shown in Table 9, complex entrepreneurs are particularly likely to start ventures alone, and they are also unlikely to be involved in low-growth sales or professional practices. Both make sense. With multiple patterns they can cover more of the business, either sequentially or concomitantly, without going outside for skills; partners are less likely to be necessary. Also complex entrepreneurs want to grow an organization; private practices are thus not fully satisfying.

If these conclusions are compared with the four basic entrepreneurial patterns in Tables 1, 3, 5, and 7, the sales and professional practice numbers look much the same. Entrepreneurs of all four types and with varying degrees of complexity all are predisposed toward growth, not the restricted size of a practice. However, the predisposition of complex entrepreneurs to start-ups without partners stands out. Personal Achievers, Supersalespeople, and Real Managers are not like this. Expert Idea Generators are much closer to complex entrepreneurs, but this would be expected because they have a strong desire to implement their own personal visions. Successful complex entrepreneurs are drawn to the independent initiation of their ventures in disproportionate numbers, and the multiple patterns available to them suggest that this is as it should be. Put simply, they are less likely to need partners, so why have them.

The case of Richard Posa of C. S. Kimeric Inc. and CSK Technical

Table 9   HOW COMPLEX ENTREPRENEURS
BECOME ENTREPRENEURS

Started Firm Without Partners	35%
Started Firm With Partners	14
Purchased Firm	11
Took Over Family Firm	27
Initiated Corporate Venture	5
Was Turnaround Person in Corporate Venture	5
Started Sales or Professional Practice	3
Total	100%

shows how complex entrepreneurs utilizing multiple routes concomitantly can independently develop a venture. His firm is both an independent start-up and an independent buyout. Posa uses both the Selling and Idea Generating Routes, consistent with his strong patterns; this has been true from the beginning. As the firm grows he is trying to become more of a visionary and to play down his own personal selling. He is not a Real Manager, knows that, and has taken steps to deal with it.

Richard Posa of C. S. Kimeric, Inc. and CSK Technical

Posa began his career after community college with a firm owned by his father-in-law, a firm specializing in water treatment. Although he came up primarily through sales and marketing, he also learned a lot about the technical end of the business. Ultimately he used a leveraged buyout to purchase from his father-in-law the Industrial Division of Buffalo Water Specialists, Inc. and started C. S. Kimeric, Inc. This involved the assets of the commercial/industrial division of the company and included a Culligan franchise to install, provide follow-up service, and issue technical support for Culligan water-treatment products. Subsequently he started his own firm as well, called CSK Technical, to manufacture customized water treatment equipment. The company produces liquid treatment systems for water and wastewater. Sales are in the industrial, government, power, and transportation industries. Systems are custom designed, typically placed on-site, and are very technologically sophisticated; usually they are computer controlled. CSK Technical has both engineering and manufacturing divisions, operates in a number of states, and to some degree internationally.

CSK Technical, with its own products and systems, has been growing very rapidly, at something like 30 percent a year. It is now up to almost $5 million a year in sales and is quite profitable. C. S. Kimeric, Inc. had some years where its sales were in the $1 million range, but recently sales have been down from that. Still the total operation is up. It has some 25 employees and is doing well. This is clearly a very high growth business overall.

As an entrepreneur Posa exhibits a degree of complexity. He is characterized by both the Supersalesperson pattern, consistent with his past and present sales orientation, and the Expert Idea Generator pattern, consistent with the highly technical nature of his business. He is about average among entrepreneurs as a Personal Achiever and as a Real Manager.

Posa gets a great deal of satisfaction out of maintaining friendly relationships with people. He is concerned about what others think and feel. Helping people is important. He is the kind of person who encourages others to participate in the decision-making process and enjoys working with a group where expertise is shared. Situations where he has an opportunity to meet people and interact with them are attractive. Not surprisingly he considers selling to be a very important aspect of his business.

This is the Supersalesperson part, but it exists beside the Expert Idea Generator pattern—not a common combination. Posa is an idea person who likes to introduce new approaches. In many ways his business is in high technology and he likes the sophisticated, innovative approach that this implies. Solving new problems is fun, and this means being flexible, open, and often imaginative. At the same time he is not one to put his company at risk. There is a delicate balance between his enthusiasm for new ideas and his commitment to follow only those ideas that he is sure will work, based on his technical know-how.

Consistent with his Supersalesperson pattern, Posa has been very successful in the sales field throughout his career. Although he is not convinced that is the way it should be, he has in fact been writing 60–70 percent of the business for some time. Yet he knows that the firm cannot continue to grow at the same rate based on his sales alone. What he sells is often big ticket in nature, like the $1.2 million contract he signed recently, but there is a limit to what he can do without help. The company is using externally contracted sales representatives, and they produced some $2 million in business last year. The internal sales effort has now been structured as a team operation with each team consisting of a technical specialist, a support staff member, a sales account executive, and a contract negotiator who is Posa himself. Thus he serves on every sales team. He hopes this team effort will spark a greater return from the in-house salespeople.

Posa is not in fact a Real Manager, and as the firm has grown he has come to see his need for help in that regard. His solution has been to hire a general manager with a strong corporate background to take over engineering, production, field operations, and administration, as well as to spearhead the development of a quality program involving a move to ISO-9000 certification. He has also strengthened his financial support staff to deal with a backlog in the company's financial statements. All this permits Posa to focus on sales and marketing, and R&D, where his strengths are greatest—and to be the visionary as the company grows.

This visionary role is something he likes, consistent with his Expert Idea Generator pattern. It was his idea to promote CSK Technical as a firm that designs, builds, installs, operates, and rents complex integrated systems competing in both the fresh and wastewater treatment markets. With a strong technology base and turnkey capabilities, the company is able to occupy a market sector that is growing dramatically. Posa is exploring the international market and many new technologies. He has an advanced approach for extracting contamination from the ground more efficiently and is pursuing a working relationship with the government under a CRADA program with the National Laboratory to expedite several new technologies. He has no problem hiring people with the expertise he lacks, but he himself has come a long way in developing a substantial amount of expertise on his own. He has taken many courses in technical areas, in sales, and in general management. Posa is very much on top of new developments in his field and uses this knowledge to find new opportunities.

SUCCESS ON THE MULTIPLE ROUTES OF A COMPLEX ENTREPRENEUR

Table 10 deals with the degree of success achieved by the complex entrepreneurs—all 38 of them—in the group of 100 established entrepreneurs, compared to the 27 entrepreneurs who showed no strong pattern.

Most of the complex entrepreneurs' companies have grown a lot, and complexity clearly provides insulation against any type of failure. The comparison to the people without a strong pattern is dramatic. And the 46 per-

Table 10   THE SUCCESS OF COMPLEX
ENTREPRENEURS' FIRMS VERSUS THE FIRMS
OF PEOPLE WITHOUT ANY STRONG PATTERN

	Complex Entrepreneurs	*No Strong Pattern*
Entrepreneur and Firm Stayed Together		
Firm Has Grown a Lot	46%	0%
Firm Has Grown Some	27	22
Recession Has Hurt Firm	3	15
Firm Has Only Survived	0	30
Entrepreneur and Firm No Longer Together		
Left Firm and Started New Venture	5	0
Left Firm and Had Non-entrepreneurial Career Subsequently	3	11
Insufficient Information Available	16	22
Total	100%	100%

cent of complex entrepreneurs in the "Firm Has Grown a Lot" category far outdistances that for the Supersalespeople (30 percent) and Expert Idea Generators (37 percent) as set forth respectively in Table 4 in Chapter 4 and Table 8 in Chapter 8. It is not as distinctive, however, when compared to the figures for the Personal Achievers (52 percent) and Real Managers (43 percent) set forth respectively in Table 2 in Chapter 2 and Table 6 in Chapter 6.

There is a good reason for this. Personal Acheivers are complex entrepreneurs 86 percent of the time. The 52 percent rate of very-high-growth firms is thus strongly influenced by their high amount of complexity.

Similarly, Real Managers are complex entrepreneurs 82 percent of the time, which influences the 43 percent rate of very high growth firms.

However, Supersalespeople and Expert Idea Generators are complex entrepreneurs only 48 percent and 67 percent of the time, respectively. This lower rate of complexity appears largely responsible for the lower frequency of high growth firms.

The importance of multiple patterns can be documented also by comparing firm success levels to the number of strong patterns the entrepreneur possesses. For entrepreneurs with three or four strong patterns—people like

Leon Smith at Niagara Lubricant—almost all of the firms are to be found in the "Firm Has Grown a Lot" category. For entrepreneurs with two strong patterns—people like Richard Fenton at Fenton, Weber, & Jones and Richard Posa at CSK Technical— there is still a heavy concentration of firms in the top category, but the next category, "Firm Has Grown Some," begins to fill up as well. The other four success categories have only a scattering of firms. In contrast, for entrepreneurs with only one strong pattern, the most frequent single category is "Firm Has Grown Some." And there are many more instances in which damage was done by recession or the entrepreneur and firm parted ways. The few cases in which the "Firm Has Only Survived" occur among entrepreneurs with one strong pattern. There is absolutely no doubt that the more strong patterns an entrepreneur has, the better the prospects for entrepreneurial success.

Earlier in this chapter, the case of Leon Smith of Niagara Lubricant illustrated the sequential use of entrepreneurial patterns, with emphasis shifting from the Personal Achiever and Supersalesperson patterns to the Real Manager and Expert Idea Generator patterns. Now let's see how sequencing works for complex entrepreneurs with two strong patterns— the Real Manager plus some other; the cases of Richard DiVita and Joseph McDougall provide examples.

Richard DiVita of the DiVita Group of Companies

For many years DiVita, with a professional degree from Canisius College, operated an accounting practice that served many small businesses. Gradually he began collecting companies and running them. Some he bought, some he started, some he has operated with one or more partners, and some have been subsequently sold. The accounting practice itself ultimately came to reside in the latter category. The DiVita Group is a holding company that over the years has maintained ownership in a wide range of enterprises including hotels and restaurants, electrical distributorships, real estate ventures, fluid power distribution firms, car washes, gas wells, and financial consultants. The most recent additions are a machine shop, a hotel and conference center, and a small inn and restaurant. DiVita has his children and other relatives in management positions in many of these companies. In most cases he holds at least a 51 percent interest.

Earnings from these holdings have fluctuated considerably. At present, sales are running at over $21 million a year and there are some 300 employees. The company is sufficiently diversified so that when one company is facing a downturn in business, others take up the slack.

There have been failures in the past, but the successes far outweigh them. Overall this has been a highly profitable small conglomerate for a number of years.

The patterns that distinguish DiVita and characterize his personal style are those of Personal Achiever and to a lesser extent Real Manager. These factors are clearly evident in the way he runs his holding company. He is above the entrepreneurial average as a Supersalesperson as well, but this factor is less pronounced, and it is less manifest in his business, although certainly not nonexistent.

As a Personal Achiever DiVita is strongly oriented toward personal accomplishment, desires information on how well he is doing, and likes to plan for future goal achievement. He is a person who predicates his behavior on the assumption that what he does is what really makes a difference. Although he is in an overall sense rather relaxed, he thinks about the problems of his company constantly and finds it difficult to unwind. He constantly looks for opportunities that he can exploit in some way. More than anything else he is a self-starter. He enjoys learning whatever is related to the success of his business and is indeed fully committed to both his profession as an accountant and his firm. Consistent with his desire for at least 51 percent ownership, he wants to make his own decisions and certainly does not wish to turn control over what he does to others. In short, he wants to be his own boss.

On the Real Manger side, DiVita manifests a number of strengths. He is a take-charge person who enjoys being in control. He is a highly competitive person who wants to win. Exercising power over others is something that he is comfortable with. Standing out in situations where he makes presentations or rises above others around him is attractive. Perhaps consistent with his accounting background, doing the routine, day-to-day things that managerial work requires comes rather easily. All in all he has many of the characteristics of an effective manager. In addition he is a rather social person who appreciates the role of a sales force in a business. Furthermore, he enjoys helping people in any way he can, especially members of his family.

The Personal Achiever pattern is most manifest in the multiple businesses, the buying and selling, the starting and shutting down, the juggling of family members into and out of various companies as appropriate. There is a great deal going on here every day. Plus there are partners to deal with in various businesses, and new business opportunities to consider all the time. Part of the strength of all this comes from the fact that DiVita owns a considerable amount of real estate and other assets. He talks about letting go and turning the various businesses over to his children, but he keeps getting into new business ventures at the same time. This does not yet sound like a person who is ready to smell the roses.

As a manager DiVita's greatest strength comes from his highly analytical background in accounting. He develops and uses a wide range of financial controls. The result is that he knows exactly how every business is doing all the time. When there is any evidence of decline, he is in a position to cut costs immediately. There are clear plans for each business and any departure from plan brings action. Because he is so knowledgeable regarding the financial aspects of his businesses, he is able to take steps to keep taxes to a minimum. Sales and acquisitions are based on well-managed information systems. Furthermore, DiVita has no problem in cutting costs and personnel when this seems needed. Yet he also know how to pump more money into a venture when the data appear to warrant it. This is how he remains competitive and profitable with a diversified industry base containing an array of companies, none of which with the exception of the restaurants that were his original family business, are within his area of special expertise.

DiVita started as a professional, but his strong Personal Achiever tendencies rapidly carried him into entrepreneurship, and ultimately out of his accounting practice completely. As his group of businesses grew, now to some 300 employees, managing this diverse array became more and more essential. That is where the Real Manager characteristic came to dominate his behavior. It has now been quite some time since he shifted gears from being a predominantly Personal Achiever to a Real Manager, who uses sophisticated information systems to guide his small empire. However, the fact that he could handle this transition within himself has been a major factor in the smooth growth of his businesses overall.

Joseph McDougall of Advanced Environmental Services

Advanced Environmental Services was founded by McDougall, a Ph.D. biologist, shortly after he served as project manager for the City of Niagara Falls on the widely publicized Love Canal case involving soil and groundwater contamination. The firm provides sampling, evaluation, and laboratory analysis of water, wastewater, soils, sediment, sludge, hazardous waste, petroleum products, and air samples. Clients are industrial and government organizations as well as professionals such as engineers and lawyers concerned with regulatory compliance and environmental responsibility. Through consultation the company designs programs to meet special environmental concerns. Services are provided by a customer services group, the laboratory, field service teams that do sampling, and an industrial hygiene unit concerned primarily with air pollution. Total quality performance is a constant emphasis.

The company now has over 500 clients in Western and Central New York state. Sales per year were bumping up against the $2.5 million mark when the recession put a real crimp in the whole industry. At that point there was a plateauing of what had up to then been a steady pattern of growth. More recently, however, the situation has improved and Advanced Environmental Services is once again in a growth mode. Throughout this period the number of employees has remained between 40 and 50. The majority owner of the business is McDougall himself, although several family members own shares as well. It has been a quite profitable operation.

Two patterns emerge from McDougall's psychological analysis— that of a Real Manager and that of an Expert Idea Generator— although he is above average as a Personal Achiever as well. The net result is a very strong multiroute thrust. He is on the one side a very practical person with a great deal of concern for efficiency, speed, and structure. Rules and procedures are important, consistent with the strong regulatory concerns of his business. He likes to hold positions of leadership and power. Winning is important. So is engaging in activities that place him at the center of the action such as making presentations, selling to a client group, or dealing with subordinates. Leadership just comes naturally. In this context he has a real supervisory talent and a very strong desire to achieve success in the leadership role. On balance his approach to selling is managerial.

Yet there is a totally different side to McDougall that manifests itself in the technical aspects of his business and in his professional background. He is original, even creative, within his field of expertise. Ideas for change and innovation come easily to him. He considers a wide range of alternatives and keeps an open mind for a long period before settling on a course of action. Thus he tends to spend a great deal of time thinking both about technological advances that he might implement and new business niches that he might exploit. Being very intelligent, he often gains a considerable competitive advantage by putting his mind to these problems. He is not one to be outgunned by the competition, at least to the extent intellectual ideas are the key to success. Yet he is not one to go out on a limb either. He is drawn to car racing, and to that extent is something of a risk taker, but in his business he is much more conservative.

Going back to grade school and the Boy Scouts, McDougall has been a leader. Currently reporting to him are managers who cover clerical activities, quality assurance, quality control, two laboratory divisions, field services, marketing and sales, information systems, and industrial hygiene. He does manage a hierarchy and he does it well. His goals for improving this managerial system include better financial management, developing the business planning side, and more evaluation of business strategies. He is taking steps to manage his accounts receivables and to increase the training effort. McDougall has a number of family members in his business, and this stretches his managerial skills because of the potential for conflict between business necessities and family loyalties. Yet he handles this situation well.

Overall, however, he still feels he is more of a professional than a manager and needs to learn a great deal in the latter respect. This is not to say he does not want to learn; quite the contrary. But at the same time he continually explores professional advantage. He is looking into new approaches to laboratory information management systems and the reduction of errors. He is constantly weighing alternative diversification approaches. One diversification has been the expansion into industrial hygiene, which has achieved some success. Another that has been implemented is ongoing landfill monitoring. There is the possibility of diversifying into Mexico and Europe, forming partnerships, and generally extending the range of field crews and sales offices. Upgrading the technology is a constant concern and a source of major investment as well. The firm strives to develop and utilize technological improvements and innovations. McDougall has even thought about instituting a day-care center. The ideas constantly keep coming, and many of them ultimately get managed into fruition; the result is further company growth. Throughout it all McDougall is very much in charge.

The venture initially engaged McDougall's Expert Idea Generator pattern almost entirely. Here was a Ph.D. biologist with many ideas entering into a newly created industry that was far from being well defined at the time. There was plenty of room to think your way to success. But as the company grew, and a network of regulations became established, there was a need to manage further growth. Again, having the Real Manager pattern within himself served McDougall well. People like this do not have to rely on others to get the managing done. It comes naturally to them at the point where it is needed.

AN ALTERNATIVE APPROACH TO COMPLEXITY

Although complexity is usually defined as being the possession of multiple patterns, there is an alternative approach: adding up the scores on all four patterns (as spelled out in Chapter 10 and Appendix B) and then using this combined score to establish whether complexity is present. This approach assesses the overall strength of a person as an entrepreneur.

When this alternative approach is used, the rate at which firms succeed is even more striking than in Table 10: the proportion of firms in the "Firm Has Grown a Lot" category increases to 55 percent from 46 percent, and no firms are found in the "Recession Has Hurt Firm" and "Firm Has Only Survived" categories. On this evidence, I feel that those who score high on this alternative measure are complex entrepreneurs. When complexity is defined using this alternative method, however, it does not change anything I have said about complexity when complexity is defined by multiple patterns. I use the alternative approach only as a supplement, to add to the number of complex entrepreneurs.

THE TRAPS THAT FACE COMPLEX ENTREPRENEURS

In Chapters 2, 4, 6, and 8, I discuss the traps for the four basic types of entrepreneurs and the antidotes for the traps. There are no special traps for complex entrepreneurs. So if you are a complex entrepreneur, you may have any one of a number of combinations of strong patterns, and what these patterns are determines what traps you face.

When there are more patterns there are more traps, but there are also more ways of reaching success. It is essential, however, to understand yourself and to behave accordingly. For example, if you are a Personal Achiever and a Real Manager, you must know that in order to know the traps and their antidotes.

Failure comes with not following at least one of the routes appropriate to your strong patterns. Conversely, if you fail to follow (for whatever reason) a route for which you have the talent as a complex entrepreneur, you still have at least one other route available to you; thus, getting caught in a trap on one route does not necessarily mean failure for complex entrepreneurs.

CONCLUSION

Complex entrepreneurs possess more than one strong pattern, and thus have the potential to follow more than one route. The more patterns they possess, the greater their likely success, but having three patterns is rather uncommon, and four is rare.

Among the 100 established entrepreneurs I studied, complexity occurs about 40 percent of the time. A Personal Achiever or a Real Manager have a very good possibility of having an additional entrepreneurial pattern. Supersalespeople are much less likely to be complex entrepreneurs. And remember that being a complex entrepreneur occurs much less frequently among the general population than among the established entrepreneurs in my research.

Multiple patterns may be utilized effectively in two different ways:

1. Sequentially—One pattern may be emphasized in the firm's early period, and then largely displaced by another pattern as the firm grows. Thus, the entrepreneur changes from one route to another over time.

2. Concomitantly—Two or more patterns, and routes, are activated at roughly the same times, and the entrepreneur continually shifts back and forth.

Complex entrepreneurs are particularly likely to start their own ventures without partners; with a wider range of talents, partners are less necessary. Complex entrepreneurs are in a very good position to grow ventures rapidly. And their chances of experiencing real adversity are very low. Furthermore, the more strong patterns they have, the more routes are available, and the better the chances of substantial success.

This matter of complexity, sequential and concomitant use of patterns, multiple patterns and routes, and increasing probabilities of success is new. I know of nothing in past treatments of entrepreneurship that deals with such issues. Yet the ideas involved are very powerful. They work to explain and predict venture success better than any other approach I know of. Consequently, it is important to incorporate complexity in any process of assessing entrepreneurial potential. Whether people are attempting to determine their own potential or assessing the potential of another person, such as a possible partner or someone whose venture is a candidate for investment, they must move beyond estimates of individual patterns to obtain a broader picture using the complexity idea.

CHAPTER 10

Assessing
Entrepreneurial Talent:
Your Own and Others'

In previous chapters I discussed the personality patterns of successful entrepreneurs and the career routes required to realize their potential. I have not, however, spelled out how you might determine your own entrepreneurial potential or, if appropriate, determine the potential of another person with whom you are contemplating, or are, doing business.

This chapter presents several procedures to assess entrepreneurial talent. I begin with the easiest and most direct—a self assessment using your own insight and judgment. Later in the chapter I consider assessments using psychological tests and questionnaires.

HOW TO ASSESS YOURSELF

To aid in your self assessment, I have developed a form, which is shown in Exhibit 1. This Self Assessment Form is based on the battery of tests used to assess the entrepreneurs discussed in this book; the only difference is that this form relies not on test scores, but on your personal judgment and insight.[1]

The Self Assessment Form has Rating and Assessment Sections. You first rate yourself in terms of the characteristics of the Personal Achiever, Supersalesperson, Real Manager, and Expert Idea Generator. These are the same characteristics discussed in Chapters 1, 3, 5, and 7. Second, you compare your score to the standards needed to qualify as one of these entrepreneurial types.

Let me first explain how to complete the Self Assessment Form and then illustrate this with an example.

The Rating Section

The Rating Section has four steps.

First, for each characteristic, make a judgment about yourself on a three point scale:

- Very Much—A person exhibits a characteristic with a great deal of consistency. This equates to the "Very High" category used for the cases in Chapters 1 to 8.
- Sizable—A person exhibits a characteristic somewhat less than "Very Much," but still to a degree that is well above average. This equates to the "High" category in the cases in Chapters 1 to 8.
- Less—A person exhibits a characteristic somewhat less than in the "Sizable" category. People in the "Less" category may be below average, average, or even somewhat above average in the characteristic; but they do not disply it as obviously as people rated as "Very Much" or "Sizable." Only people who obviously have a characteristic are credited with it—and end up in the "Very Much" or "Sizable" categories. The "Less" category equates to the "Not a Factor" category in the cases in Chapters 1 to 8.

Because the "Less" category extends over a much greater range than the others, a person who is not yet a successful entrepreneur usually will have more checks in this column than in the others.

As you can see from the form, it is just a matter of putting a check mark in one of the three columns that follows each characteristic.

The second step involves totalling the check marks in each column.

Third, multiply the total in each column by 2, 1, or 0 as indicated on the form. This simply weights the scores with 2 for "Very Much," 1 for "Sizable," and 0 for "Less" (that is, Not a Factor).

Fourth, for each characteristic, add the weighted score for the "Very Much" and "Sizable" columns. Then transfer this total to the Assessment Section in the first column.

The Assessment Section

For each entrepreneurial type, compare your score with the numbers in the second column, which are the standards developed using the group of 100 established entrepreneurs. If your score for an entrepreneurial pattern equals or exceeds the standard in the second column, put a check mark in

Exhibit 1   SELF ASSESSMENT FORM

Rating Section

	Degree Characteristic		
	Very Much	Sizable	Less
Personal Achiever Entrepreneur (See Chapter 1 for definitions and examples)			
1. Need to achieve	_____	_____	_____
2. Desire for feedback	_____	_____	_____
3. Desire to plan and set goals	_____	_____	_____
4. Strong personal initiative	_____	_____	_____
5. Strong personal commitment to their organization	_____	_____	_____
6. Belief that one person can make a difference	_____	_____	_____
7. Belief that work should be guided by personal goals, not those of others	_____	_____	_____
Number of checks	_____	_____	_____
	$\times 2$	$\times 1$	$\times 0$
	_____ +	_____	$0 =$
Personal Achiever Score	_____		

	Degree Characteristic		
	Very Much	Sizable	Less
Supersalesperson Entrepreneur (See Chapter 3 for definitions and examples)			
1. Capacity to understand and feel with another	_____	_____	_____
2. Desire to help others	_____	_____	_____
3. Belief that social processes are very important	_____	_____	_____
4. Need to have strong positive relationships with others	_____	_____	_____
5. Belief that a sales force is crucial to carrying out company strategy	_____	_____	_____
Number of checks	_____	_____	_____
	$\times 2$	$\times 1$	$\times 0$
	_____ +	_____	$0 =$
Supersalesperson Score	_____		

Degree Characteristic

	Very Much	Sizable	Less
Real Manager Entrepreneur (See Chapter 5 for definitions and examples)			
1. Desire to be a corporate leader	_____	_____	_____
2. Decisiveness	_____	_____	_____
3. Positive attitudes to authority	_____	_____	_____
4. Desire to compete	_____	_____	_____
5. Desire for power	_____	_____	_____
6. Desire to stand out from the crowd	_____	_____	_____
Number of checks	_____	_____	_____
	$\times 2$	$\times 1$	$\times 0$
	_____ +	_____	0 =
Real Manager Score	_____		

Degree Characteristic

	Very Much	Sizable	Less
Expert Idea Generator Entrepreneur (See Chapter 7 for definitions and examples)			
1. Desire to innovate	_____	_____	_____
2. Love of ideas	_____	_____	_____
3. Belief that new product development is crucial to carrying out company strategy	_____	_____	_____
4. Good intelligence	_____	_____	_____
5. Desire to avoid taking risks	_____	_____	_____
Number of checks	_____	_____	_____
	$\times 2$	$\times 1$	$\times 0$
	_____ +	_____	0 =
Expert Idea Generator Score	_____		

Assessment Section

		Check If Score Is at or Above Number	
Personal Achiever Score	_____	8	_____
Supersalesperson Score	_____	5	_____
Real Manager Score	_____	4	_____
Expert Idea Generator Score	_____	5	_____

Number of checks (Two or more indicates a complex entrepreneur— see Chapter 9 for definitions and examples of complexity)			_____
Alternative Complex Entrepreneur Score (Total of four scores)	_____	18	_____

column three. This signifies that you are a Personal Achiever, Supersalesperson, Real Manager, or Expert Idea Generator.

If there are two or more strong patterns equaling or exceeding the standards indicated, you are a complex entrepreneur. If you do not equal or exceed the standard for two or more entrepreneurial patterns, there is an alternative approach to determine whether you are a complex entrepreneur. Add your four pattern scores in column one. If the total equals or exceeds 18 (the standard that identifies a complex entrepreneur), you are also a complex entrepreneur. These two ways of determining complexity are not "either/or." Your total score may equal or exceed 18 and you may very well still have two or more strong patterns as well. If, however, your total score is at or above 18, but you have only one strong pattern (this turns out to be the minimum possible), you are a complex entrepreneur based only on the alternative approach—your greatest strengths are in those areas where your scores come closest to the pattern standard.

An Example of a Completed Self Assessment Form

To assist you in filling out the Self Assessment Form, a completed form is shown in Exhibit 2. Notice how the checks are totaled for each column and then multiplied by 2, 1, or 0 as appropriate. Then the results for the "Very Much" and "Sizable" columns are added to obtain the pattern score; thus, 4 + 3 = a Personal Achiever Score of 7.

The results of this process for the four patterns are transferred to the Assessment Section, yielding values of 7, 8, 5, and 4 respectively. The Personal Achiever Score of 7 is below the standard of 8, so the person, although having a high score, is not considered to possess the Personal Achiever pattern. The Supersalesperson Score of 8 does exceed the standard of 5, and the Real Manager Score of 5 exceeds the standard of 4, so these two patterns are characteristic and are checked. The Expert Idea Generator Score of 4 falls just short of the 5 needed to establish a strong pattern.

That two patterns are strong is sufficient to establish that this is a complex entrepreneur. However, the alternative approach confirms this con-

Exhibit 2   SELF ASSESSMENT FORM

Rating Section

	Degree Characteristic		
	Very Much	Sizable	Less
Personal Achiever Entrepreneur (See Chapter 1 for definitions and examples)			
1. Need to achieve		✓	
2. Desire for feedback	✓		
3. Desire to plan and set goals			✓
4. Strong personal initiative		✓	
5. Strong personal commitment to their organization		✓	
6. Belief that one person can make a difference			✓
7. Belief that work should be guided by personal goals, not those of others	✓		
Number of checks	2	3	2
	×2	×1	×0
	4 +	3	0 =
Personal Achiever Score	7		

	Degree Characteristic		
	Very Much	Sizable	Less
Supersalesperson Entrepreneur (See Chapter 3 for definitions and examples)			
1. Capacity to understand and feel with another	✓		
2. Desire to help others			✓
3. Belief that social processes are very important	✓		
4. Need to have strong positive relationships with others	✓		
5. Belief that a sales force is crucial to carrying out company strategy	✓		
Number of checks	4	0	1
	×2	×1	×0
	8 +	0	0 =
Supersalesperson Score	8		

Degree Characteristic

	Very Much	Sizable	Less
Real Manager Entrepreneur (See Chapter 5 for definitions and examples)			
1. Desire to be a corporate leader		✓	
2. Decisiveness	✓		
3. Positive attitudes to authority			✓
4. Desire to compete		✓	
5. Desire for power			✓
6. Desire to stand out from the crowd		✓	
Number of checks	1	3	2
	×2	×1	×0
	2 +	3	0 =
Real Manager Score	5		

Degree Characteristic

	Very Much	Sizable	Less
Expert Idea Generator Entrepreneur (See Chapter 7 for definitions and examples)			
1. Desire to innovate	✓		
2. Love of ideas		✓	
3. Belief that new product development is crucial to carrying out company strategy			✓
4. Good intelligence			✓
5. Desire to avoid taking risks		✓	
Number of checks	1	2	2
	×2	×1	×0
	2 +	2	0 =
Expert Idea Generator Score	4		

Assessment Section

		Check If Score Is at or Above Number	
Personal Achiever Score	7	8	
Supersalesperson Score	8	5	✓
Real Manager Score	5	4	✓
Expert Idea Generator Score	4	5	

Number of checks (Two or more indicates a complex entrepreneur—see Chapter 9 for definitions and examples of complexity)			__2__
Alternative Complex Entrepreneur Score (Total of four scores)	__24__	18	__✓__

clusion. The sum of the four pattern scores is 24, which far exceeds the minimum standard of 18.

Avoiding the Tendency to Overrate Yourself

A particular strong pattern is found only among the top quarter to one-third of *established* entrepreneurs; strong patterns do not occur nearly as frequently in the general population. This is important to remember because there is a tendency for people to overrate their own attributes. This tendency has been studied most extensively in connection with performance appraisals, where self-appraisals can be compared with evaluations by others, such as superiors.

Self-appraisals are not of much use for evaluative purposes such as decisions on compensation and promotion. They tend to be highly inflated, with almost everyone speaking well of themselves.

The Self Assessment Form is much like self-appraisal of performance in that many performance appraisal forms include questions dealing with personal attributes of much the same kind as the characteristics noted in the Self Assessment Form. What reason then is there to believe the self assessment approach can identify entrepreneurial talent? Research shows that when used for developmental purposes to stimulate problem solving and receptivity to suggestions, self-appraisals have more value.[2] The Self Assessment Form is helping you engage in this career development process, and so I believe it to be a useful indicator of entrepreneurial talent.

A tendency does exist for people who want to view themselves as entrepreneurs to inflate their own scores and thus emerge on the Self Assessment Form with stronger patterns than a test battery would give them. You can counteract this tendency, however, by closely reading this book, including the descriptions of characteristics and the case examples. You are not trying to get a raise or a promotion; you are trying to help yourself. No one else even has to know how the process turns out. The Self Assessment Form is only providing a systematic method of organizing your own insights. If it is completed carefully, it can prove useful. If it is not, it can be misleading.

With this in mind, I suggest that after you complete the Self Assessment Form you go back over the self-ratings just to be sure you have not overstated your entrepreneurial potential. If you think overrating of this kind has occurred, make the necessary corrections.

Using the Self Assessment Form to Assess Others

You can use the self assessment form to assess others in whom you have a business interest and who you know well: partners or potential partners, and their fit with the needs of a venture; potential successors in a family business, most frequently children; potential staff for a corporate venture; and applicants for venture capital. In addition bank officers can assess loan applicants and better assess the risks, and guide a venture in a manner consistent with the entrepreneur's capabilities. Managers in government entities with the mission of economic development and fostering small-firm growth can evaluate those they might support. There are other similar situations as well. The key requirement is that the assessor know enough about the person being assessed to carry out a meaningful and valid evaluation.

People in these situations do in fact utilize personality factors in making investment decisions of various kinds. This is well established.[3] But it has been much less common to do this in any systematic manner, as the Self Assessment Form would require. Yet it is reasonably easy to take the form and use it to assess another person about whom you have accumulated considerable information. Furthermore, third parties can be drawn on to provide outside input to these decisions, again in a more systematic manner than simply asking "Does this person have entrepreneurial talent?" In short, if you are going to use information about personality characteristics in any event, this is a systematic method of doing so that can produce useful and comprehensive results.

INCORPORATING TESTS AND QUESTIONNAIRES IN THE ASSESSMENT PROCESS

In addition to the Self Assessment Form discussed, there are two other ways to assess entrepreneurial talent. One is quite simple—various published measures are used to aid the self assessment process. The other is much more complex, and involves the use of tests and questionnaires as part of a comprehensive professional assessment.

Using Published Tests and Questionnaires

In books and sometimes in magazines and newspapers, there are tests or questionnaires dealing with some facet of the person or the venture, which when completed tell a person where he or she stands on the particular factor measured.[4] These tests and questionnaires do not deal with everything involved in the four entrepreneurial patterns discussed in this book, but they can inform you about some of the component characteristics—things like creativity and innovation, risk taking, need for achievement, and locus of control.

Once you complete them and score them, these measures provide direct feedback on some factor assumed to be related to entrepreneurial success. This simplicity makes them appealing. However, these indexes may not always measure what they are supposed to measure. They look as if they do, and the factors considered would appear to be important for a successful venture, but research regarding the validity of these indexes is rarely available. Consequently published tests and questionnaires of this kind should be treated with caution.

Using Professional Feedback

Professional feedback utilizes tests and questionnaires selected and administered by a professional. The measurements are relatively free of bias and thus objective, and if used well and based on considerable knowledge of the person, they can provide comprehensive information. This process overcomes potential weaknesses inherent in self assessment, such as overrating. Furthermore, it can allow for two-way communication, thus permitting better understanding, and more informed decisions, than are usually possible with self assessment.

Whether professional feedback yields sufficient benefit to justify the added cost is an individual matter. Usually I suggest starting with self assessment, and if the results leave a person with a continuing sense of uncertainty, then move to professional feedback. The types of tests used in professional feedback are noted in Appendix B.

When you are investing considerable time, effort, or money in another person who is, or might have the potential for being, an entrepreneur, the arguments for some type of professional assessment become even stronger, especially if the person is not well known to you. If the consequences are substantial, I would want all the information possible about the entrepreneurial capabilities of such a person.

The professional feedback consultant requires two kinds of data.

1. The person being assessed must complete a number of tests and questionnaires bearing on the four patterns and the personality characteristics inherent in them. This can take as long as four hours, and some people may find it taxing.

2. The person being assessed, or a third party, must provide information regarding the existing venture, if one exists, or the venture plan or vision, if the venture does not as yet exist. This plan or vision may be very detailed or quite fuzzy; it is still important. The information about the existing or projected venture should, to the extent possible, cover:

   A. Background (history, products and services, markets, firm size, nature of the industry)

   B. Firm Structure (organization table, various individual roles, physical plant, ownership, professional support)

   C. Financial Data (sales, balance sheet, profit and loss, cash flow, capital expenditures)

   D. Venture Goals (short and long term, priorities)

   E. Major Problem Areas (dimensions, origins, company impact, possible resolutions)

   F. Significant Opportunities (nature, source, potential impact, resources needed)

Once the test data and business information are in hand, the professional analyzes them, preparatory to carrying out a one-on-one feedback session. I can best illustrate what happens in these sessions with an example in which I was the professional consultant.

Example of a Feedback Session

An entrepreneur had an existing business that he had founded several years before with three partners. His major concern was a spin-off he was contemplating that would manufacture and market a new product that he had invented. From my discussion with him the following list of problems emerged:

1. How should the entrepreneur market the new product?

2. If the entrepreneur manufactured the new product, where should he focus his own efforts, and what skills should he hire?

3. How should the new endeavor relate to the existing business and to what extent should the other partners be involved?

4. Did the entrepreneur personally have what it took to persevere with his invention and bring it through to market?

I started the feedback by describing the test results. The entrepreneur demonstrated a high need to achieve, no matter what measure was used. He also had a strong desire to innovate, consistent with his inventor mentality and the creation of new businesses. However, he did not appear to be strongly motivated as a planner, which could create problems.

The entrepreneur's scores indicated that he did not like to take a high level of risk, and this risk avoidance was consistent with what we knew about successful inventor-entrepreneurs. Also, his locus of control was heavily internal, with very little feeling of any external influences either from powerful people or chance circumstances. He was a *Type A* personality to the point of being somewhat addicted to stress. Questions about his health indicated no evidence of current health problems, however.

Insofar as intelligence was concerned, the entrepreneur appeared to be quite capable of meeting the challenges he faced. He had a real empathy for people and a potential talent for sales; in my discussions with him he strongly supported this conclusion.

The entrepreneur scored high on several measures of managerial talent. He was a take-charge person and appeared to work well with authority. Unlike many entrepreneurs, he seemed to have the capacity to manage growth and develop an organization of substantial size. He did not possess professional motivation to any marked degree.

He appeared to determine his own work outcomes and seemed to like it that way. Hierarchical, professional, and group processes were less significant for him than working where he could do his own thing.

I then repackaged these test results, using the four personality patterns. As a Personal Achiever, the entrepreneur had many strengths in areas such as strong achievement motivation, internal locus of control, Type A personality, and a high value placed on personal goals and individual accomplishments. Yet, among other things, he was not a planner and did not particularly enjoy new learning, nor did he possess an especially strong sense of commitment. Overall he was above average as a Personal Achiever, but this was not a really strong pattern.

The Supersalesperson pattern was strong, however. His feeling for others and his desire to help them were the main contributors, but there were other strengths here as well. The Selling Route was clearly one he should follow.

As a Real Manager, he had many positive characteristics of a corporate leader, plus positive attitudes to authority and a desire to exercise power.

This was a strong pattern; managing was in his repertoire of skills and I encouraged him to use those skills.

Finally, and not surprisingly for a demonstrated inventor-entrepreneur, a strong Expert Idea Generator pattern was in evidence. He liked to introduce innovative solutions, was concerned about new product development, had a rather high level of intelligence, and did not like to take risks. Along with the Selling and Managing Routes, the Idea Generating Route was also open to him. I explained the concept of a complex entrepreneur, and I told him he had that type of talent.

Applying these results to the problems identified earlier, I told him that he clearly could create and grow a new venture of the kind he had in mind. Given his proclivity for working with people and understanding their needs, plus this type of business' critical need to generate sales and cash flow initially, he must concentrate first on selling his product, and hire skills in the financial and manufacturing areas. He appeared comfortable with such an agenda. I advised him that later on, as the business grew, it would be best to assume a more general managerial role.

The biggest threat to the whole endeavor could be a lack of planning, which in turn might mean a failure to coordinate various functions. I advised him either to devote his energies to overcoming his distaste for planning or to hire someone who could help in this regard. The latter might be more realistic.

The test data did not clearly indicate how the new endeavor should be related to the existing company except to suggest that the entrepreneur operate as independently as possible. Clearly he wanted to, and could run his own show. But he was capable of working with others, even those with authority over him. Thus, this was not a major area of concern. Personality considerations could be subordinated to existing business realities in this area.

Throughout the feedback session, the discussion focused on business problems and entrepreneurial characteristics, not test titles and measured scores. As I discussed each characteristic, I gave the entrepreneur an opportunity to provide substantiating data and to raise questions as well. From this a great deal of support for my interpretations emerged. The entrepreneur did, however, question the conclusion that he lacked professional motivation. He explained why he felt differently, and we discussed his strong desire to help others, which indeed is one of the characteristics of professionals. I made no attempt to force my interpretations on him, only to provide such information as the assessment process yielded.

As the session wound up, two hours after it began, I gave the entrepreneur a chance to raise any questions that might be answered from the assessment data. He returned to the problem of planning, which he clearly recognized as a source of difficulty. He remembered several instances from his past where a failure to plan had gotten him into trouble. I told him that recognizing weaknesses like this when they appear can often help people find ways to overcome them. I told him that if he wanted to talk more about this later on we could do so.

Obviously every feedback session is different, simply because the people differ. Yet all should be structured along the lines of this example.

CONCLUSION

I strongly urge you to use the Self Assessment Form to determine your own entrepreneurial talent. You may want to use it as well to assess the talents of others. Recognize that there is a perfectly natural tendency to overrate yourself. Try to keep that tendency from distorting your ratings. Be sure you fully understand the characteristics on which you are making your ratings. That requires a thorough reading of earlier chapters.

If for any reason this self assessment process does not produce results with which you are fully comfortable, there is an alternative: career development assistance from a professional. This requires completing tests and questionnaires, and providing detailed information on your current or projected venture. To conduct these assessments and the feedback sessions, a professional must have knowledge of personality measurement procedures and of how businesses, especially entrepreneurial businesses, operate. It is important that both types of expertise be present.

Finally, if the Self Assessment Form does not indicate any strong pattern for you, and yet you still feel pulled toward entrepreneurship, take heart. Chapter 13 discusses alternatives for people who lack strong patterns.

NOTES

1. This type of approach in self assessment is not new. It is used by Jeffry A. Timmons, for instance, in his book *The Entrepreneurial Mind.* Timmons suggests rating yourself on a number of characteristics that researchers, venture capitalists, and practitioners believe to be important for entrepreneurial success. However, he does not focus on the four key personality patterns of entrepreneurs.
2. The research in this area is discussed in much greater detail in my book with Donald P. Crane titled *Human Resource Management: The Strategic Perspective.*

3. The book *New Venture Performance* by William R. Sandberg documents this conclusion at some length.
4. Tests and questionnaires of this kind are contained in *The Woman Entrepreneur* by Robert D. Hisrich and Candida G. Brush, *Entrepreneurship* by Robert D. Hisrich and Michael P. Peters, and *Organizational Entrepreneurship* by Jeffrey R. Cornwall and Baron Perlman.

CHAPTER 11

Do Women Possess Different Patterns and Follow Different Routes?

Along with real similarities, real differences exist between men and women entrepreneurs. These differences are important, and I will explain them in this chapter. But first, it may help to place women into some historical context as to entrepreneurship.

For many years entrepreneuring, like managing, was considered the province of men. That is no longer true. Although in the past most businesses were started by men, the ratio has gradually shifted over the past 25 years so that now women are starting twice as many new ventures. As a result of this increased rate, women should own half of the businesses in the United States within 10 years.

However, this does not mean that the total sales volume of women-owned businesses will equal that of firms owned by men, although the figures are getting closer. One factor is that the women-owned businesses are newer and thus have not had time to grow as much. Also, many of the firms that women start are part-time or seasonal ventures. Finally, and this may prove most important in the long run, most women (currently about 90 percent) start service businesses, not manufacturing operations. Their firms are heavily concentrated in sales, consulting, design and architecture, public relations and advertising, and personnel and business services. Retail stores, travel agencies, real estate firms, and the like are most frequent. In many of these cases, the market served is highly localized and the growth potential is somewhat limited.

In addition to the different types of businesses started by men and women, some research indicates personal differences as well: women have less business and technical education than men, have interests that may restrict their entrepreneurial prospects, have more limited business networks than men, and are less likely to have some personality characteristics that contribute to entrepreneurial success.[1] These findings establish quite definitively that male and female entrepreneurs differ, and they explain some of the differences in entrepreneurial behavior between men and women. Yet there are numerous descriptions of outstandingly successful women entrepreneurs, and these confirm what many have long suspected: there are no inherent limits on what women can do as entrepreneurs.[2]

There are a great many gaps in what we know about women entrepreneurs and the differences in entrepreneurial skills between men and women. Women who are, or want to be, entrepreneurs do not have much information to go on. I can improve on that situation. Among the 100 established entrepreneurs whom I studied, 12 were women. My conclusions about women entrepreneurs are based in part on this group, but also on other research, our own and that of others; these conclusions provide some important guidelines.

HOW WOMEN AND MEN GET STARTED

Table 11 shows the origins of the ventures started by the 100 established men and women entrepreneurs.

Women are much more likely than men to start a business with a partner (or several partners). In the great majority of these instances, a husband is a partner. This fits with the findings from other studies as well. Sometimes the husband remains involved; sometimes because of death or divorce, the woman takes over the firm completely. More often than not the husband is a positive force, and a major source of support, but not always. I know of cases where the husband is contributing to major problems that the business faces.

Partners can bring needed skills and expertise to a business. So the high frequency of partners for women in Table 11 does not signify any inherent deficiency in skills or talents; it may well be a transitional phenomenon, and as women receive more business and technical education the need for this sharing of the reins will decline. I know of women who have experienced partnerships and now swear that they will never have a partner again. And many women go on to grow substantial firms on their own. One woman whom I know, after her husband's death, took their small publishing house to the very top of its field, doubling its sales many times over. Family members, and husbands, are like other partners—some help the business and some do not, some are needed in the business and some are not. There is nothing wrong with building from what others have accomplished, or

Table 11   HOW WOMEN AND MEN
BECOME ENTREPRENEURS

	Women	Men
Started Firm Without Partners	8%	23%
Started Firm With Partners	50	17
Purchased Firm	18	11
Took Over Family Firm	8	25
Initiated Corporate Venture	8	7
Was Turnaround Person in Corporate Venture	0	10
Started Sales or Professional Practice	8	7
Total	100%	100%

helped to accomplish. Any partner should be looked at in terms of their potential contribution. Husbands are no different in this regard.

As Table 11 shows, with partnership start-ups more frequent among women, sole start-ups are lower. This is not surprising. However, other forms of venture origin are lower as well. Fewer women are selected to head a family business. These results, obtained with our rather small group of women entrepreneurs, are supported in other studies.[3] Often sons are raised to take over the family business, especially the first-born son, and daughters are not. As a consequence the daughters leave the business for other careers at an early point, or stay on in positions where they exert little influence. Talent may matter very little in these situations. In the past most businesses have been transferred to daughters only when no sons were available, if then.

I believe this will change. For one thing more women-owned businesses are likely to mean more opportunities for succession by daughters. We see some evidence of this already. Also, as more women obtain business education and experience the whole context of deciding on a successor can change. Then perhaps the possession of entrepreneurial talent—the needed patterns and the fact of complexity—will influence succession decisions more.

In addition to fewer women than men taking over family businesses, Table 11 indicates that women are unlikely to enter into a corporate venture and serve as a turnaround person. A major factor here appears to be that fewer women possess the particular types of business skills and experience required for this role at the present time. Again, however, change is occurring. Also the Expert Idea Generator pattern required to be an effective turnaround person appears to be less frequent among women entre-preneurs. I discuss this factor later in this chapter.

My study of MBA students provides further understanding on business origins. When we followed up on these students after graduation, we found that 25 percent of the men were engaged in some type of entrepreneurial activity, versus 10 percent of the women. This suggests a greater tendency for men to pursue an entrepreneurial career. However, women tend to start their firms at a later age than men. Since in our study both women and men were of the same age, the women would be expected to accelerate their rate of firm formation relative to men, as they move further beyond graduation. Thus I do not believe these results mean women are any less entrepreneurial.

ACHIEVING SUCCESS THROUGH COMPLEXITY

Table 12 shows how well the 12 women and 88 men among the 100 established entrepreneurs have done. The women are distinguished by a higher proportion of firms in the "Firm Has Grown a Lot" category and by the complete lack of firms in the two less successful groups—"Recession Has Hurt Firm" and "Firm Has Only Survived."

If you compare the percentages in Table 12 with those in Table 10 in Chapter 10, you will see that the women in Table 12 look more like complex entrepreneurs, and the men more like people without any strong pattern. This suggests that complexity may be more characteristic of the women. This hypothesis is confirmed. The women were more likely to have multiple patterns, especially three strong patterns. And when the alternative approach to measuring complexity is used, two-thirds of the women qualified as complex entrepreneurs.

Thus, women may well have a very high level of entrepreneurial talent. And they should be able to attain the very highest levels of entrepreneurial success. Furthermore, as Table 12 shows, the women, in fact, outachieve the men.

These are, of course, women from a very special group. Certainly, in the population as a whole, this amount of entrepreneurial talent will not exist for women, any more than it does for men. Yet seeing how these women have engineered their careers is illuminating. Jacqueline Taylor of Stovroff and Taylor Travel, whose case example is described in Chapter 1, is both a Personal Achiever and a Supersalesperson who has followed the Achieving and Selling Routes to grow her firm very rapidly.

Brenda Calhoun of Calhoun Insurance Agency and Lupé Breen of Dun-

Table 12   HOW THE FIRMS OF
WOMEN AND MEN SUCCEEDED

	Women	Men
Entrepreneur and Firm Stayed Together		
Firm Has Grown a Lot	33%	20%
Firm Has Grown Some	18	25
Recession Has Hurt Firm	0	13
Firm Has Only Survived	0	9
Entrepreneur and Firm No Longer Together		
Left Firm and Started New Venture	8	6
Left Firm and Had Nonentrepreneurial		
Career Subsequently	8	6
Insufficient Information Available	33	21
Total	100%	100%

hill of Buffalo and Dunhill Temporary Systems are examples of women who possess three strong patterns. Consider how they went about preparing themselves for, and achieving, entrepreneurial success.

Brenda Calhoun of Calhoun Insurance Agency

Calhoun Insurance is a minority-owned and -operated business that got started primarily by writing substandard automobile insurance (for drivers who would not otherwise qualify for insurance) through companies that specialize in this type of insurance and the New York State Risk Plan, which is required to provide auto insurance to anyone who holds a valid license. Now the firm writes business insurance, especially for construction companies, and insurance for nonprofit organizations such as churches, as well as a wide range of personal lines such as homeowners, automobile, and valuable items floaters. A small percentage of the business is in estate planning. Basically this is a broadly diversified insurance agency specializing in commercial, but also with personal lines as well as life and health products.

Before starting her own agency, Calhoun worked primarily in underwriter positions, but also occasionally as an account executive, for a number of companies including Kemper Insurance and Fireman's Fund. Her credentials are impeccable. The firm she created has grown steadily and is now up to almost $1.5 million in sales per year. The number of employees is currently at seven and growing. The firm has a large number of customers, but many are at a rather low dollar volume. Much of the company's current business situation reflects its operation, in large part, within the minority community, a community that at least in the Buffalo area provides a limited market.

Calhoun's psychological profile is impressive. More than anything she is a Personal Achiever, where she scores unusually high. She is also very high as a Real Manager and as an Expert Idea Generator. This is a true triple-threat person with tremendous entrepreneurial drive. As a salesperson, however, she uses primarily a hard-sell, managed approached. Her background has been more in underwriting than in sales.

If we look at the Personal Achiever pattern, the things that really stand out are a high level of achievement motivation, a distinct desire for feedback on how well she is doing in the form of such things as increased sales, a clear interest in planning and setting goals for the future, and a feeling that results achieved are not so much a matter of luck as of her own efforts. Calhoun is really involved in her work and lives with her problems day and night. She has a great deal of initiative. She wants to learn whatever her business demands, and in fact she has taken many professional insurance courses above and beyond her college degree. She really wants to determine for herself what her work will consist of; turning things over to a group of people who work for her is not her idea of fun.

As yet Calhoun does not have many people to manage, but she is a Real Manager nevertheless. She likes to take charge and run things; such managerial functions as directing the work of subordinates come easily to her. She is very self-assured, has a strong desire to be successful, wants to put her talents to use, and is not in any sense insecure—quite the contrary. All of these qualities tend to make for effective managerial performance. There is every indication that she runs things well.

Finally, there is the Expert Idea Generator side of Calhoun. She loves to start new things and introduce changes. She is a very intelligent person and this helps her in finding new directions for her business; she simply outthinks the competition. But beyond this, she possesses a conservatism, a tendency to take risks only if the odds are almost certainly in her favor, which constrains her enthusiasm for her ideas and introduces an element of caution. She is an idea person, and a good one, but within limits imposed by the realities of the situation.

All three of these patterns are manifest in the way Calhoun approaches her business. She is doing a thousand things at once, she has all kinds of ideas for growth and new niches, and she not only manages everything herself, but she is trying to expand her operation to be able to manage even more. She describes her duties as account procurement and development, in addition to agency growth and development. That takes in a lot of ground. The company handles a wide range of insurance products and represents a number of different carriers. Calhoun is trying to obtain direct appointments from the insurance companies, thus increasing her commission income, and has had some success on that score; she is trying for more of these appointments. She is working to obtain capital for growth—probably a line of credit. She is looking for a person who could team up with her in the pension business, about the only type of line she does not now have.

Plans are under way in a number of areas. Key to much of this is the introduction of a computer system that will track clients and transactions, putting clients on direct billing. Calhoun hopes to expand this system to set up a procedure for providing servicing to a network of agents. She already has 10 who are interested. She is thinking of moving to a more upscale location in the city and also of expanding into a new suburban niche. She has contracted with a telemarketing firm to help in the selling end. Some might view all this activity as indicative of a lack of focus, yet Calhoun has very good reasons for all the things she is doing, and it is her nature to have many ideas in various stages of development at the same time. What to others might be a serious overextension, is to her simply keeping herself fully challenged.

Brenda Calhoun possesses the Real Manager pattern to handle growth, but a sequential use of her multiple patterns has not occurred, at least not yet. The problem is that the company is not yet large enough to require full-scale managing, and Calhoun already has the Personal Achiever capability to operate a venture of the current size. The result is that her Real Manager pattern has been diverted into managed selling. At the same time, as an Expert Idea Generator, she is working to find the vision that will propel her venture into more rapid growth. Thus, she is currently using all three patterns at once—the Personal Achiever pattern to operate and continue to grow the enterprise, the Real Manager pattern to consummate sales, and the Expert Idea Generator pattern to find new niches for growth. If all this works out as it should, Calhoun will be devoting most of her energies to managing a much expanded business in a few short years. Then the sequential use of patterns will occur.

Lupé Breen of Dunhill of Buffalo and
Dunhill Temporary Systems

This is a franchise business, part of the worldwide Dunhill organization, which consists of over 300 franchises. Dunhill of Buffalo was
originally purchased by Breen from the estate of her former employer.
Some years later she started Dunhill Temporary Systems, which spe-
cializes in the placement of temporaries, rather than the employment
agency operations of the original business. A small royalty and a fee for
advertising are paid to the parent organization by the franchises.
Although both companies would qualify for designation as a minority-
owned business, on the basis of their owner's Hispanic origins, the
benefits of this designation have not been utilized.

The two companies complement each other in a number of ways.
Clients that receive permanent placements often utilize temporaries as
well. Temporaries are often hired permanently after a trial, and a conversion fee is realized at that time. The temporary firm focuses now on
secretarial, accounting, bookkeeping, data entry, word processing, and
specialized office support personnel, and is by far the major money
producer. Clients include financial service firms, diversified manufacturers, real estate brokers, law firms, and hospitals. The list contains
most of the major companies in Western New York. The business has
grown quite rapidly from a very low dollar volume of sales at the time
of purchase to over $2.1 million a year for both firms. The in-house
staff has stayed around 10, but there are now 100 temporaries working
in client companies. Although there have been unprofitable years, this
is the exception; overall, profits have been quite respectable.

Breen has a very strong entrepreneurial profile. She is first and
foremost a Supersalesperson, but she also is an Expert Idea Generator
and a Real Manager. All of these characteristics manifest themselves in
her career and in the way she has grown her firms. She really wants to
help other people and does this by solving their human resource
staffing problems. She enjoys being involved with people and exhibits
a great deal of warmth, kindness, and feeling in her relationships with
them. She does not like disagreements; there is a tendency to see the
best in others even when this requires leaning over backwards on her
part. Her strategy for her firm includes a strong emphasis on selling.
All this is entirely consistent with the Supersalesperson pattern.

Like many Expert Idea Generators, Breen is strong on innovation.
Solving new problems is fun, doing the same thing over and over is not
fun, and sharing power with others is no problem. She likes to find

new options for her businesses by searching out a wide range of alternatives. She is intelligent, which helps her in developing ideas for change; she is enthusiastic, but not to the point of becoming so enthused about her ideas that she takes excessive risks.

Finally, Breen is a Real Manager who has a talent for getting people to follow her views on what directions the business should take. She can be decisive, wants to do the things needed to achieve success, enjoys utilizing her talents to the fullest, and is very secure personally. All this makes not only for the capacity to manage her employees, but also to manage the sales process as well, when that seems called for.

How have these entrepreneurial strengths played out as the two Dunhill franchises have grown? Selling has been Breen's strong point. Although she has been more effective in some areas than others, overall she has been very good at business development. Part of her strategy has been to become widely known in the community through professional activities, service on boards of various kinds, and work with women's groups. She has a wide network of influential friends, which has ultimately contributed to the growth of her business.

As an idea generator Breen has been a constant source of innovation. Originally the firm was heavily concentrated in professional placement. The newer strategy has been to shift much more into office services, and this has worked well. In an effort to complement her own strengths she has brought in partners in both businesses. This too has proved to be a very good idea. Satellite offices have been opened to capitalize on alterations in sources of business. A new computer system was introduced. There has been a shift in the customer base with greater emphasis on premier clients with whom both services and margins can be increased. In an effort to remain competitive, the companies have introduced screening procedures that test for grammar, spelling, mathematics, and the like. Changes are occurring constantly as Breen adjusts to and often heads off alterations in the marketplace. The start-up of the temporary company was just one of many such innovations.

As a manager Breen has been very effective. An example stems from the early days. When she bought the business originally, three of the top counselors in professional placement left immediately to form their own agency, and a fourth left to have a child. Yet somehow she was able to hire replacements and manage the business through the crisis to produce a small profit even in this first year.

Lupé Breen followed the Selling Route when she first bought the business and it was small; she still does a good deal of selling through her networking.

But as the company has grown to surpass 100 employees, there is more and more to manage. Breen's Real Manager pattern has been increasingly called into play. In addition, throughout her entrepreneurial career she has been an innovator, in the tradition of Expert Idea Generators, constantly generating ways to achieve competitive advantage.

Calhoun and Breen are three-pattern complex entrepreneurs who also, as with all such entrepreneurs I have studied, prove to be complex using the alternative approach to establishing complexity. The case example that follows is different in several respects. First it deals with a nontraditional type of entrepreneurship for women. Second, it presents a case of complexity where only one clearly strong pattern exists, but based on the alternative approach, the individual is without question a complex entrepreneur. Margaret O'Connor has much overall strength, even though only her Expert Idea Generator pattern is really strong. This is an illuminating case, simply because it is so different from those of other female entrepreneurs I have considered.

Margaret O'Connor of Air Charter Service

Air Charter Service was formed when O'Connor and her husband purchased the assets of a prior company. Air Charter Service flies passengers to destinations extending from New England to Michigan and as far south as Washington, D.C. In addition to the charter business operating from its Western New York point of origin, the firm acts as an aircraft broker by getting airplanes to fill company needs, provides aircraft management by handling planes for companies, and serves as an air ambulance when people need an organ transplant. A small proportion of the business involves handling cargo. Most customers are business people and professionals.

The company has six employees including four pilots. It does close to $400,000 in annual business now and in a few short years has become profitable. It is expanding steadily. Peggy O'Connor is the majority owner, president, and visionary. She grew up in aviation, both of her parents being pilots. For nine years she worked for American Airlines as a flight attendant, supervisor, and emergency procedures training instructor.

O'Connor is particularly strong as an Expert Idea Generator. That is her number one entrepreneurial pattern and fits with her role as company visionary. However, she is well above the entrepreneurial average on all three of the other patterns as well. As an idea person she is constantly generating new ways of doing things and innovative solutions to company problems. She loves the challenge of thinking her way to competitive advantage. Among her talents is a keen capacity to judge the abilities and potential of other people. Thus she is able to develop her plans for change in ways that factor in the strengths and weaknesses of others. Compromise, when necessary, is no problem. She tends to look at the big picture and to leave small details to others. Timing is important to her, and she gives a great deal of thought to exactly when it would be best to undertake specific initiatives. She wants to win very much, but she is willing to bide her time and wait for opportunities. Thus she is far from being a gambler; it is important to think things out so that any risk is reduced to the barest minimum.

Although Air Charter Service started by owning its own plane, it has now shifted to a strategy whereby it utilizes the unused time of planes owned by corporations. This leasing approach has given the company a sizable cost advantage and permits a schedule of charges that is not only below that of the competition, but permits significant margins as well. Since adopting this strategic thrust, the company has grown very rapidly. Much of this growth has been created by a marketing and sales campaign that has tripled the customer base and become a model for an industry that until recently has lacked innovative approaches in this area.

There have been a number of other changes, many of them unusual for a company this size. A computer now provides instant price quotes. Ground transportation for passengers (rental car, taxi, or limousine) is arranged in advance and confirmed by radio from the aircraft prior to landing. A turbo jet has been added to the fleet recently, which because it can fly to destinations more rapidly than the planes of competitors, has generated a considerable amount of new business. The organ transplant business in particular has increased. The company is consolidating what previously were dispersed operations at the Niagara Falls Airport. A bid has also been submitted to manage that airport. Things are indeed moving very rapidly. O'Connor is looking into a number of other opportunities as well, including a major expansion into Canada and building facilities, some of which would be rented out, at the Buffalo Airport. She is thoroughly enjoying the process of seeing her ideas become realities.

NOT HAVING AN EXPERT IDEA GENERATOR PATTERN

Based on the 100 established entrepreneurs, and the three case examples, nothing suggests that women lack the Expert Idea Generator pattern. But other data contribute to a different conclusion.

Based on these latter data, I am convinced that women entrepreneurs are somewhat less likely than men to be Expert Idea Generators.[4] Women are found less frequently among high technology entrepreneurs. I find them less involved in venture turnaround efforts as well. In other areas they may well be the equal of males, but the overall numbers suggest that women entrepreneurs are somewhat less innovative, and thus less entrepreneurially talented in this particular respect, than their male counterparts. I speak here of women as a group. Obviously any individual woman can be an Expert Idea Generator and be as innovative as any individual man.

Given this, do women have a greater chance of failure as entrepreneurs than men? I think not. First, women entrepreneurs appear more likely than men to be complex entrepreneurs, and thus *more* likely to succeed. Second, nothing indicates a real difference between women and men on any of the other three patterns—Personal Achiever, Supersalesperson, or Real Manager. Finally, the ventures in which women are most likely to be involved suggest they are following the career routes most appropriate to their strong patterns. They are in the services, and less involved in invention and high technology. Their routes appear to match their patterns. As long as they follow the routes appropriate to their strong patterns, women should have the same chance of entrepreneurial success as men.

CONCLUSION

I find some rather marked differences between women and men with regard to entrepreneurship:

1. Women are more likely to start businesses with partners, less likely to take over a family business, and less likely to be a turnaround person in a corporate venture.
2. Women start entrepreneurial activities immediately after receiving the MBA degree less frequently than men, reflecting the tendency for women in general to start ventures at a somewhat later age.
3. Complexity is more frequent among women entrepreneurs, and this contributes to somewhat higher levels of entrepreneurial achievement than among men.
4. While women and men are equally likely to be Personal Achievers, Supersalespeople, and Real Managers, women do not possess the Expert Idea Generator pattern as often. This should make little difference as long as appropriate career routes are followed.

There may be remaining problems insofar as business networks, obtaining financing, and the like are concerned, but from a talent perspective, if appropriate routes are followed, women and men are equally capable of achieving entrepreneurial success. In exactly the same way men do, women need to assess their own personality patterns and structure their plans for success and thus the routes they follow. The outcomes may be different, because the patterns are not identical, but the process required is the same. If women possess the necessary capabilities, I can find no reason why they should not plunge into entrepreneurial ventures in increasing numbers. Furthermore, since these capabilities are in most cases not age related (except for the Expert Idea Generator pattern that women are somewhat less likely to have), I would encourage an early plunge. The quicker women get into entrepreneuring, all else being equal, the more time they have to enjoy it.

NOTES

1. This evidence is discussed in *The Woman Entrepreneur* by Robert D. Hisrich and Candida G. Brush, as well as in *Women-Owned Businesses*, edited by Oliver Hagan, Carol Rivchun, and Donald Sexton.
2. Examples are provided by Lloyd Shefsky in his book *Entrepreneurs Are Made Not Born*.
3. J. L. Ward in the book *Keeping the Family Business Healthy* indicates that only one-third of family firms continue to the second generation, and less than 15 percent continue to the third. Yet even within this limited context, succession involves male children much more often than female.
4. This conclusion is based primarily on a study by Renato R. Bellu of 50 successful women entrepreneurs in the New York City area published in the journal *Entrepreneurship and Regional Development*.

CHAPTER 12

Educating for Entrepreneurship

At numerous points throughout this book I have discussed the ways that education and training can contribute to entrepreneurial success. Now I want to focus on this topic in more detail, simply because it is so important. Because they operate with much uncertainty in uncharted waters, entrepreneurs have a huge need to acquire information about themselves and their environments.[1] As this learning progresses, uncertainty turns into certainty, and unmanageable situations become manageable. Education is the means through which much of this learning occurs.

In this chapter I discuss the types of education and training that work best for entrepreneurs with different strong patterns, education, and training that can help them follow the Achieving, Selling, Managing, and Idea Generating Routes, as appropriate. I will give attention both to formal, degree programs in business schools and to more limited nondegree programs.

SHOULD I PURSUE A BUSINESS DEGREE?

I am often asked whether I would recommend pursuing an MBA to prepare for an entrepreneurial career. My answer is—If you can find an MBA program concerned directly with entrepreneurship, by all means pursue it. The problem is that very few programs of this kind exist. At most, 25 universities in the United States make a portfolio of entrepreneurship courses available, and these programs still contain a majority of required courses that are not of an entrepreneurial nature.

In fact, most MBA programs prepare students for corporate careers.

Where entrepreneurship is taught, and it is certainly increasingly taught, it tends to be somewhat peripheral. For example, courses are frequently taught by individuals with entrepreneurial experience, who are neither educated in nor writing in the entrepreneurship field. Furthermore, many universities have a very small, although often enthusiastic, faculty in the area. They are therefore vulnerable to rapid staffing changes. When a professor who has been promoting entrepreneurship leaves, there may be little left behind, and courses and programs suffer. In most universities, entrepreneurship is a highly popular, volatile, and not fully integrated field, which is decidedly secondary to the corporate thrust that permeates most courses and is the subject of most faculty writing and research.[2]

A few programs are entrepreneurial enough for me to recommend, but even these can change rapidly. Thus the key question really is whether the typical, corporate-oriented MBA degree is of any value to a present or prospective entrepreneur. That depends on the person, on which strong patterns they have, and on the route they are trying to follow.

To help you decide, the remainder of this chapter presents a number of case examples in which an MBA contributes in varying degrees to a subsequent entrepreneurial venture.

I also want to describe the extent of entrepreneurial talent in the typical business school that focuses primarily on a corporate mission. The MBA program at SUNY Buffalo is of this type.

Table 13 compares the prevalence of the four patterns among the 150 students in my elective entrepreneurship course (the only course on the subject available to SUNY Buffalo MBAs) and the 100 established entrepreneurs. The figures for the MBA students are well below those for the established entrepreneurs on three of the four patterns. Only on the Supersalesperson pattern did the students exceed the established entrepreneurs. In addition, complexity, as noted in Chapter 9, is considerably less prevalent among the MBA students. (In Table 13 the columns do not total to 100% because some entrepreneurs and students lacked any strong pattern and others had multiple patterns.)

The SUNY Buffalo type of MBA program, with its strong corporate emphasis, is not attracting the kind of people who become successful entrepreneurs. The only exception is the Supersalespeople, and these may well go on to corporate careers in marketing, not entrepreneurship.

Table 14 summarizes what we found when we followed up on the students after graduation.

The key finding: A high proportion of the Personal Achievers entered some type of entrepreneurial activity shortly after finishing the degree. There are not many of them, and a number of the ventures are only part

Table 13   STRONG PATTERNS AMONG
STUDENTS AND ENTREPRENEURS

	MBA Students	*Established Entrepreneurs*
Personal Achievers	10%	29%
Supersalespeople	38	27
Real Managers	10	33
Expert Idea Generators	25	33

Table 14   SUBSEQUENT ENTREPRENEURIAL
ACTIVITY AMONG THE MBA STUDENTS

Personal Achievers	60%
Supersalespeople	29
Real Managers	46
Expert Idea Generators	31
Complex, Multiroute Entrepreneurs	52

time, but the attraction to entrepreneuring is clearly evident. In contrast, Supersalespeople and Expert Idea Generators are attracted at only half the Personal Achiever rate. This propensity for entrepreneurship can be put in perspective by examining the students who had none of these strong patterns; only 4 percent became entrepreneurs, and all of them on a part-time basis. Thus having a strong entrepreneurial pattern makes a difference.

While a corporate-type MBA program may not attract a sizable amount of entrepreneurial talent, it definitely does not stifle the entrepreneurial drives of those it does attract. It can help a person to become more successful by making it easier to follow the appropriate route.

Just as Personal Achievers, Supersalespeople, Real Managers, and Expert Idea Generators must pursue different career paths to success, each will gain something different from formal degree programs and nondegree developmental courses. Accordingly, each must be examined separately.

EDUCATING PERSONAL ACHIEVERS

Personal Achievers prefer a focused learning—learning related directly to what the venture requires. The cases of Arnold Benson and John Jaski show how two Personal Achievers used an MBA and an MBA/law degree combination in their ventures. (The names of the students in these and subsequent cases are not their real names.)

MBA Student Arnold Benson

Arnold Benson graduated with an MBA in marketing. His undergraduate degree is in engineering.

His predominant Personal Achiever pattern is reflected in very strong achievement motivation, a desire for feedback on achievements, an internal locus of control coupled with an expectation that external influences from powerful people or circumstances will not operate on him, a hard-driving personality that generates considerable stress, a desire to find out information and learn, and a strong sense of commitment to his organization. A very high value is placed on work in which personal goals, individual accomplishments, and the demands of the task itself govern; a lesser value is placed on work in which a peer group governs. No other pattern is nearly as strong as that of Personal Achiever, although Benson is above the entrepreneurial average as a Supersalesperson and as a Real Manager.

Benson owns a distributor/manufacturing concern purchased with a partner prior to entering the MBA program. The business has expanded into retailing since and has been organized so as to encompass several separate corporations. Benson wants to diversify into a variety of business ownership positions. His MBA was intended as a method of learning how to do this.

Although he undoubtedly has had to learn a great deal in the MBA program that was not relevant to his goals, something that is very frustrating to Personal Achievers, it is also true that with an engineering background he had much to learn about business. Thus, overall, the degree did contribute to his goals. This kind of learning can also be obtained through direct experience; that, however, usually takes much longer.

MBA Student John Jaski

John Jaski pursued a degree program that gave him both a law degree and an MBA. His undergraduate degree is in political science, and he operated a small business in the construction industry while an undergraduate.

As a Personal Achiever, Jaski is characterized by very strong achievement motivation, a desire to plan and set goals for future achievements, an especially pronounced internal locus of control that is tied to a belief that external chance events will not exert an influence, and the type of personality that yields a lot of stress. Although this Personal Achiever pattern is clearly dominant, all three other patterns are above the average for entrepreneurs.

Jaski has opened a solo/law practice, having been admitted to the bar prior to completing the MBA. Although on the surface this might appear to represent a professional private practice, there are several factors that dispel this impression. For one thing, the practice operates in tandem with another solo practice in another city; thus it is already expanding. Second, Jaski has every intention of growing the current practice through the addition of both support staff and other lawyers. Finally, he has opened a retail bookstore not far from his law office. Clearly this is a professional who is expanding into entrepreneurship. In the process he is making effective use of both his legal and his business education.

In the short term the legal education is more relevant. However, as Jaski diversifies into other businesses beyond his profession, the MBA can add increasing value. Without doubt he could have fulfilled his needs by taking selected business courses, rather than the full MBA program. Nevertheless, having an MBA surely does him no harm.

Entrepreneurship Development for Personal Achievers

Formal degree programs take considerable time. Often Personal Achievers can learn what they need through short courses that focus on practical applications. In addition I recommend two other types of training to Personal Achievers:

1. Achievement motivation training. This training helps you to develop achievement motivated behavior—problem solving, goal setting, business planning, risk handling—through specially designed business games. Personal Achievers experience both the anxieties and satisfactions of setting and achieving personal and business goals, with these experiences linked to real-life situations through practice. Obstacles that might hinder attaining goals are closely evaluated. Participants consider sources of feedback on goal

attainment as well, and learn to understand their strong motives that relate to achievement.[3]

2. Training in business plan preparation. These courses take a variety of forms, but almost always the end result is preparation of a plan—either to obtain financing for a new venture or to operate an ongoing business.[4]

Because achievement motivation and the desire to plan are critical characteristics of Personal Achievers, training such as that described above develops the talents of these people.

EDUCATING SUPERSALESPEOPLE

Developing formal courses to teach selling in schools has always been difficult because so much of the learning must be product or service specific. You have to develop knowledge about what is being sold in order to sell it. But because products and services span such a wide range, it is difficult to create a college program that is relevant to the diverse interests and needs in a given class. On the other hand, company-operated programs have no such problems. Thus, degree programs, such as the MBA, usually are not very useful to Supersalespeople. But let's see how two Supersalespeople—Gloria Sosa and Brian McKee—used the MBA and a doctoral degree.

MBA Student Gloria Sosa

Gloria Sosa has earned an MBA in marketing. Her undergraduate degree is in accounting, and she is a CPA.

Although consistent with her accounting background Sosa possesses strong professional motivation, she has the Supersalesperson pattern of an entrepreneur. She has a good capacity to feel with others, plus a highly positive orientation to people, and she also has a very strong desire to help others. She has a concern for the sales force as an instrument of company strategy, ranking that factor number one in her company among various competitive strategic thrusts. No other entrepreneurial pattern is particularly significant.

Sosa operates her real estate development business while continuing to work as a CPA in an accounting firm and to teach accounting at a community college. Thus her entrepreneurial activity is part time and it is with a partner. She started the business while in graduate school.

Originally it had an equity interest in apartment complexes that it managed. More recently it has moved into home construction. Sosa handles financial matters for the firm, but she is also increasingly involved in marketing and customer relations.

The value of the MBA to Sosa is not clear-cut. I sense that her move from accounting to the sales and marketing thrust that characterizes the MBA is of recent origin but is continuing. If this route is followed consistently the results should be favorable and the MBA education could prove useful. At this point it is too early, however, to determine whether her Supersalesperson pattern and the career route as reflected in the MBA will gel completely. Even if they do, it is uncertain how important the MBA learning might be to any sales success.

Ph.D. Student Brian McKee

Brian McKee has been working toward a doctoral degree in entrepreneurship. He completed his coursework several years ago, and is just now finishing his dissertation. His undergraduate degree was in psychology.

He is a very strong Supersalesperson possessing a good feeling for and understanding of people, as well as a pronounced desire to help others. He is also well above the entrepreneurial norm as a Personal Achiever, although not quite to the point where this pattern can be said to be really strong. Based on his score using the alternative approach, he is nevertheless a complex entrepreneur.

McKee does not aspire to start a business at this time. Yet he provides a good example of how an entrepreneurial propensity can manifest itself in teaching and/or research in the field. He has been involved in a number of research endeavors involving entrepreneurship, including several international studies he has conducted. After completing his degree McKee intends to teach entrepreneurship at a university and to assist others in starting businesses. Thus, there is a definite link between his education and his present and intended career.

I find that faculty members in the entrepreneurship area often do have a personality profile consistent with actually becoming an entrepreneur. Many have in fact started businesses. I remember attending a conference of teachers of entrepreneurship where this matter came up. A show of hands indicated that a great majority had at one time or another started a business. Thus, it is not surprising that McKee's degree work in entrepreneurship is consistent with his career intentions. However, nothing indicates that it allows him to follow the Selling Route better.

Entrepreneurship Development for Supersalespeople

While formal degree programs are of questionable value to Supersalespeople, I do, however, recommend two kinds of training:

1. Company sales training. Supersalespeople should experience at least one company sales training course, preferably a course closely related to the venture you have in mind; the products or services should be similar. If at all possible, participate in several such courses.
2. Sensitivity training (a.k.a. laboratory training, team building, and participative management training). Without exception, programs of this kind are intended to teach participative management and how to move power and authority down in the business structure to the level of the work group. Thus the entrepreneur is expected to give up a degree of control and operate in a group setting. For Supersalespeople this is no problem at all; they are generally quite responsive to this type of training.[5]

These types of training, like those for the Personal Achievers, bring out or enhance the strengths of the entrepreneur's specific pattern.

EDUCATING REAL MANAGERS

Real Managers can have successful corporate as well as entrepreneurial careers, and managing is a skill that can be enhanced in formal degree programs. The cases of Norma Uleman and David Haas show two Real Managers using MBA degrees to follow the Managing Route.

MBA Student Norma Uleman

Norma Uleman has an MBA in marketing with a good background in accounting and computers as well.

She is predominantly a Real Manager who tends to be directive in style, likes competition, desires to exercise power, and desires to differentiate herself from others around her. She is well above the entrepreneur average on all three other patterns as well. She would have to be considered a complex entrepreneur, even though only the Real Manager pattern really stands out.

Uleman started a business providing bookkeeping services on a mobile basis to small and mid-sized companies. It was a highly computerized operation. The business continued for some time subsequent to the award of her MBA, but when she moved to another city, she terminated the business. She now has entered the corporate world, first in sales and then in an administrative capacity. This close tie to corporate management is characteristic of Real Managers and certainly the sales orientation fits with what can be expected in these people prior to entering upon a full-scale managerial position. It is hard to say where Uleman will end up, but certainly a return to entrepreneurship cannot be ruled out. Her MBA helps her in her current management position and will also be of assistance if she follows the Managing Route in some new venture.

MBA Student David Haas

David Haas has obtained an MBA degree in marketing, with backup expertise in finance and management information systems.

He is first and foremost a Real Manager with a directive style, a very strong desire to compete, an assertive personality, a pronounced desire to exercise power, and a desire to differentiate himself so as to stand out from the crowd. At a somewhat lesser level, but still above the average for entrepreneurs, he is something of a Personal Achiever and an Expert Idea Generator.

At present Haas is a part-time entrepreneur. He sells for a financial services firm primarily, but he also participates in the family restaurant business as he has for many years, is a partner in a restaurant discounting venture, is involved in network marketing, and is in the process of starting an independent distributorship. His approach to selling is one of managing the process, and at present at least his managerial capabilities are put to use more in the sales area than in actually managing. His MBA appears to have been of value in this regard and also in providing product knowledge. It gives him a capacity to speak with expertise and authority as he enters on a sales dialogue. Like Uleman, Haas has not yet reached the point of managing a fully developed entrepreneurial venture. If he does, his MBA learning should prove even more valuable.

Entrepreneurship Development for Real Managers

For Real Managers entrepreneurship development and management development become one. Anything that aids their management skills will help them follow the Managing Route as well. I believe that two approaches are particularly useful:

1. Job rotation. In family businesses Real Managers might work their way up through various positions, learning as they go. A very effective approach involves exchanging heir-apparents with another firm for a period of time, thus providing an opportunity to learn outside the business. As a potential entrepreneur a Real Manager might deliberately put in one or two year stints with different firms. All of this is job rotation. The more they manage in the process the better.[6]
2. Training in dealing with ineffective subordinates. A variety of programs of this kind exist. The primary method of instruction is lecture and discussion. By studying methods for diagnosing and correcting the ineffective performance of subordinates, participants develop skills in decision making and controlling. In the process they come to hold new perspectives on the managerial job, and often strenghten their managerial motivation as well. On occasion case analyses are also included.[7]

Managing requires a substantial body of knowledge and considerable skill. Learning on the job and through development programs can be quite valuable.

EDUCATING EXPERT IDEA GENERATORS

Expert Idea Generators must be experts. The case of Costas Pappas shows how an MBA provided that expertise, and the case of Peter Nichols shows how an MBA served as a catalyst for using other knowledge.

MBA Student Costas Pappas

Costas Pappas grew up in Greece. His MBA is in marketing and international business. As an undergraduate in the United States he obtained a degree in business administration, but with a strong orientation to liberal arts studies.

He is, above all, an Expert Idea Generator. This involves a strong desire to introduce innovative solutions, a major commitment to developing ideas, and a compensating desire to avoid excess risks. This is the essence of an Expert Idea Generator pattern.

Pappas returned to Greece after receiving his MBA and worked for a large corporation in the treasury management area for several years. More recently he has gone on his own, leasing out yachts to the tourist trade for vacations in the surrounding waters. He has been able to locate a niche within this industry whereby he can borrow money to finance yacht purchases and still make a substantial profit. His skill is clearly in niche identification, and this skill was enhanced through what he learned during his MBA training. Pappas learned the skills of business administration to a point of expertise, then worked in finance to perfect this expertise, and only then started a venture that depends on financial know-how.

MBA Student Peter Nichols

Peter Nichols has a general MBA degree. His primary background, however, is in engineering, a field in which he has obtained several advanced degrees.

He is above anything else an Expert Idea Generator. Consistent with this pattern he has a strong desire to introduce innovative solutions, a love of ideas that yields considerable creative output, and at the same time a strong desire to avoid risks of any kind. He has a major concern for new product development as an instrument of his company's strategy and backs this up, as is typical for inventor-entrepreneurs, with the personal creation of potential products.

Nichols started a high technology company with several partners before he began working on his MBA. The MBA was intended to provide him with the business knowledge he lacked from his technical education, and it has done that. The company has been a vehicle for developing and implementing several different inventions. Nichols intends to initiate other businesses as his business knowledge and technical capabilities expand.

In this instance the primary expertise comes from outside the MBA context. The MBA is a catalyst, a special context, which helps to bring the primary expertise to the level of its full potential. It is possible that this might happen without an MBA, but having the degree can only help in cases of this kind.

Entrepreneurship Development for Expert Idea Generators

Expert Idea Generators need a substantial amount of training to bring them to expert status. This may take a variety of forms. Formal training may extend from apprenticeships to a Ph.D. program. However, in many cases there is no formal training in the particular area of expertise, and learning occurs on various jobs or through personal study. More frequently a combination of approaches is used, with different types of development used for different purposes.

An example of how this works is provided by an Expert Idea Generator who now owns a mini-conglomerate doing over $100 million in sales a year; the core business relates to security and the detection of crime. A college degree in criminal justice got him started. From there he went to a transport company where as director of security he learned the security business on the job. At the same time he attended polygraph school and learned how to become an examiner. Then he went to work for a company doing polygraph examinations. Gradually he developed his own practice, and then hired other examiners to work for him. This was his first start-up. There have been many since, providing services such as guard and patrol, investigation, polygraph training, bus transportation, drug testing, honesty testing, and support to the security, law enforcement, and corrections communities. He owns a number of office buildings.

His early ideas were for new businesses related to security concerns. As the number of these businesses grew, however, he faced the need to apply his skills to the business process in general. To assist him in this area he first took several nondegree courses at a local college and later completed the three-year Owner/President Management Program at Harvard Business School. He continues to think up, and start, new ventures. He is particularly interested in developing creative approaches to financing that do not dilute his ownership.

Clearly this individual has drawn upon many sources for his learning. Expert Idea Generators tend to do this, and it is entirely consistent with the Idea Generating Route to follow this type of approach. Learning occurs at times, and in areas, as the need presents itself.

A second approach for Expert Idea Generators is some type of training in skills and techniques of generating creative ideas, solving problems, and making decisions. This training can take a number of forms, but a common element is practice in looking at things and situations differently. Various problem-solving exercises are often used. Much of this training goes under the name "creativity training." It can help people to think in novel and creative ways, and that is what Expert Idea Generators specialize in.

EDUCATING COMPLEX ENTREPRENEURS

Because complex entrepreneurs seem to have sufficient talent to become entrepreneurial successes in any event, they may well benefit less from formal education than other types of entrepreneurs. The following cases show this.

MBA Student Louis Alba

Louis Alba has an MBA with a finance major.

He is very strong on three of the four patterns—Supersalesperson, Real Manager, and Expert Idea Generator—and comes very close to being equally strong on the Personal Achiever pattern as well. He is a complex entrepreneur.

As a Supersalesperson he is characterized by a good capacity to understand others and a very strong desire to help them. As a Real Manager he is inclined to a directive approach, possesses a strong desire to exercise power, and has a desire to differentiate himself so as to stand out from the crowd. As an Expert Idea Generator he has a desire to introduce innovative solutions, a love of ideas, and yet a substantial desire to avoid taking risks.

While still an undergraduate, Alba, along with several partners, formed a firm to provide floral designs and horticultural displays. The venture has been sufficiently successful so that he has been able to support his MBA work from its earnings. His long-term objective is to form a company to engage in international trade with the Eastern European countries. At present he is exploring opportunities and developing ideas with this objective in mind. His MBA education has proven valuable as he looks at various methods of financing this type of venture, although he also feels he needs a stronger background in international law. Thus his MBA training has only partially filled his needs for knowledge.

MBA Student Michael Tyler

Michael Tyler has an MBA degree with specialization in finance. His undergraduate work is of a scientific nature.

He is a complex entrepreneur—both a Personal Achiever and an Expert Idea Generator. (This is not a frequent combination in any of the groups I have studied.) The Personal Achiever pattern is reflected in a strong achievement motivation, a very pronounced desire for feedback on achievement, a desire to plan and set goals for future achievements, an internal locus of control that is added to a belief that chance factors exert little influence, a hard-driving personality, and a very strong desire to learn.

As an Expert Idea Generator, Tyler has a strong desire to introduce innovative solutions, an intuitive and conceptual approach that is idea-oriented, and the desire to avoid risks so as to keep his enthusiasm for his ideas under control. He is indeed a very creative person.

For some time Tyler has been engaged in inventing products for inclusion in weapons systems. Some of his ideas have been good, some he has rejected. He now has taken one such idea to the point of a patent application and the establishment of a joint venture to manufacture the product. Clearly the MBA has been of value as Tyler has negotiated with various firms to finance and produce what he has created. However, he is the kind of person who researches things and learns on his own also, quite independent of the formal educational process. Thus it is difficult to assess how much the MBA has contributed. Perhaps the inventions would have found their way to market in any event.

MBA Student Marie Gaspari

Marie Gaspari has both undergraduate and MBA degrees in marketing.

As a complex entrepreneur she has two strong patterns—Supersalesperson, consistent with her penchant for marketing, and Expert Idea Generator. As a Supersalesperson she possesses a good feeling for and understanding of people and a very strong desire to help others. In addition she views the sales force as a very significant instrument of company strategy in both her ventures. As an Expert Idea Generator she is characterized by an intense desire to introduce innovative solutions, and a very strong love of ideas.

Since finishing her MBA, Gaspari has taken a lead role in a nearly dormant family business. Her objective is to find a way to start the business growing once again. In addition she is in partnership with several other people in a financial venture that is sales based and involves working with pension funds. This latter venture is particularly attractive because it gives her considerable latitude to put her MBA and her selling skills to work. However, at this point it is not clear what route she will follow, and thus how useful her MBA will be. We may not know for some time.

Entrepreneurship Development for Complex Entrepreneurs

Although formal degrees may not be especially helpful to complex entrepreneurs, they can benefit from nondegree courses:

1. Any of the types of entrepreneurial development considered in this
   chapter can yield a substantial return to complex entrepreneurs if
   they are applied in pursuit of an appropriate route. Complex entrepreneurs are just like any other strong pattern entrepreneurs, except
   that they have more routes available and thus more types of training
   that will help them.
2. There are also entrepreneurship development programs that apply
   to multiple routes. The SUNY Buffalo program, for example, had
   the following elements:
   A policy council of experienced and very successful entrepreneurs
   A recruiting and selection process to enroll established, growth-
     oriented entrepreneurs
   A nine-month program including orientation, clinic sessions
     where participants describe their ventures, mentors, content
     symposia, book review sessions, social sessions for network-
     ing, and an assessment process to establish patterns
   Subsequent alumni activities

Because different kinds of entrepreneurs are included in this program,
complex entrepreneurs are more likely to be exposed to useful information
regarding several of their appropriate routes.[8]

CONCLUSION

At whatever career point a person takes an MBA, there is a question as
to its relevancy. Many programs require learning that is not needed, and at
least some may provide very little that is. The corporate, big business
emphasis can be a problem. Furthermore, universities that are strong on
entrepreneurship at one point in time may not be at another. An added concern is the recent emphasis on obtaining business experience after the
undergraduate degree before entering on an MBA. This makes some sense
for those who will embark on careers in corporate management, because
the MBA coursework is taken closer to the time at which it will be used in

a managerial position. However, for entrepreneurs concerned with getting into a venture as soon as possible it makes no sense at all.

Given these considerations, the decision to pursue an MBA should be taken only after some study of both the program being considered and of yourself. Does the program match well with your best career route? The MBA can represent a major contribution to your success, or a wasted several years, or something in between. In most instances it is the latter and the judgment can be difficult to make in advance. Generally the status and prestige that goes with having an MBA from a major university is less useful to entrepreneurs than to those who pursue careers in large corporations or in the elite management consulting firms. It is what entrepreneurs actually learn that matters most.

For Personal Achievers who aspire to careers where they quarterback ventures into growth and diversify into several enterprises, an MBA with an entrepreneurial emphasis can be quite valuable. It should be completed as early as possible, because only part of the learning that you need is available in school. What is available there provides a good underpinning for sorting out what additional knowledge and experience you should acquire elsewhere.

For Supersalespeople most graduate business programs are of limited value. There are exceptions, but overall it is more important to simply get out and learn how to sell. I know of no MBA program that can teach that.

For Real Managers the route to entrepreneurship often moves through corporate management. Consequently the typical MBA program is probably more useful to Real Managers than to any other entrepreneurial type. It can help you pursue the Managing Route.

For Expert Idea Generators who want to become niche exploiters, an MBA can be very useful in learning to identify niches and in figuring out how to develop them. No doubt the formal learning will need to be supplemented by solid experience, but it is a good beginning. This argues for acquiring the MBA as early as possible. The more entrepreneurially focused the program the better. For many inventor-entrepreneurs, however, you may be better off stressing your area of expertise and pursuing the Idea Generating Route that way; you can hire someone else (perhaps someone who already has an MBA) to handle what is outside your technical specialty.

For a complex entrepreneur who has multiple routes that may be followed either at the same time or sequentially, a truly venture-oriented MBA can be helpful. And if the Managing Route is available to you even the typical MBA program may yield value. Again, however, the earlier the MBA is earned, the longer time it has to work in your favor.

In any event you should always weigh any formal degree program against shorter, nondegree training. Among these approaches, I find the following most helpful, depending on the entrepreneur's strong pattern(s).

1. Achievement motivation training
2. Training in business plan preparation
3. Company sales training
4. Sensitivity training
5. Job rotation
6. Training in dealing with ineffective subordinates
7. Multiple source learning to develop ideas
8. Creativity training
9. Programs largely taught by entrepreneurs to each other that deal with the total entrepreneurial experience

NOTES

1. This process of venture learning is discussed at length by Zenas Block and Ian C. MacMillan in *Corporate Venturing.*
2. This interpretation is confirmed by the fact that major books dealing with business school education, such as *Management Education and Development* by Lyman W. Porter and Lawrence E. McKibbin and *MBAs on the Fast Track* by Phyllis A. Wallace, concentrate almost entirely on the corporate aspects.
3. Two sources describing this training and how it contributes to entrepreneurial success are an article by David Miron and David C. McClelland in the *California Management Review* and a book by David C. McClelland and David G. Winter titled *Motivating Economic Achievement.*
4. Studies dealing with the financial returns to planning are reviewed in an article by Brian K. Boyd in the *Journal of Management Studies.*
5. The positive effects of this training, if the right people participate, are described by Scott I. Tannenbaum and Gary Yukl in their *Annual Review of Psychology* article.
6. A good discussion of learning through job rotation is contained in an *International Review of Industrial and Organizational Psychology* piece by Timothy T. Baldwin and Margaret Y. Padgett.

7. An example of how this type of training may be organized is provided by my book *People Problems;* I discuss the research on this type of training in *Role Motivation Theories.*

8. A chapter by Susan Stites-Doe and myself in Abraham K. Korman's *Human Dilemmas in Work Organizations* describes this program in detail.

CHAPTER 13

What If I
Lack Any Strong
Entrepreneurial Pattern?

If you have read this far, including completing the Self Assessment Form in Chapter 10, and reluctantly conclude that you do not possess any strong pattern, you may find yourself finishing this book with a rather empty feeling. Clearly my intent throughout the book has been to help people with at least one strong pattern to better understand themselves and follow an appropriate career route. After you learn about patterns, complex entrepreneurs, and routes, coming up empty can be quite unpleasant. Doubly so, if you already are engaged in some type of venture or are giving serious consideration to an entrepreneurial career.

I do have a solution for those of you who lack any strong pattern, although there is no guarantee that it will work. It involves developing a professional or sales practice. I will explain how these practices operate, so you can determine whether this is a possible solution for you.

WHAT IS A SALES OR
PROFESSIONAL PRACTICE?

Private practices offer an opportunity to achieve independence and to experience the satisfaction of utilizing one's special skills and expertise. People in sales or professional practices want to do what they know how to do, and do well, not manage an organization. They are mostly concerned with keeping the practice in operation as a vehicle for applying their particular talents. Thus the goal of firm growth is subordinate to that of continuing survival. The firm and the individual become almost entirely one.

To at least 7 of the 100 established entrepreneurs growth seemed to have a rather low priority, if it existed at all. Their firms have less than five employees and annual sales tend to be under the $1 million figure; on occasion both the number of employees and sales are well below this. Yet some firms are quite profitable in terms of margins. These firms have not grown to any size, apparently because they are brand new or have run afoul of economic cycles. However, as I got to know these situations better, it became apparent that a growth orientation simply was not present because of either conscious decisions or unconscious factors. The individuals might well desire to sell more product or services, and they certainly did not intend to keep profitability at a low level. But the idea of building an organization staffed with employees has much less appeal. In many cases these are professionals independently practicing their professions. In other cases they are salespeople operating as independent manufacturers' representatives or selling a particular type of product or service on their own. All are involved in start-ups.

If growth-oriented entrepreneurs are contrasted with these private practitioners, what stands out is their different objectives. Those with professional practices use these practices to carry on the activities associated with their profession, many of which were learned during their prior professional education and on-the-job experience. Their primary motivations are professional in nature—to acquire knowledge and expertise; to practice independently without having someone tell them what to do; to establish a reputation as an effective professional, thereby achieving status in the field; to help clients solve their problems and achieve their goals; and to devote themselves to the standards and ethics of their profession.[1]

The same situation appears to operate among the sales practitioners. They enjoy selling, have learned how to do it quite well as a result of their prior experience, and want a work context where they are free to sell in a manner and to the extent they see fit. To them it is important not to manage the sales, or any other type of activities, of others.

There is no question that firms of this type can add value to a society, and provide wealth. What they do not do, however, is build an organization, add jobs, and grow an enterprise.

This should not be taken to imply that these practices are any less important or attractive as a source of employment. They are merely different. They offer freedom and the satisfaction of doing what you want to do. They can bring monetary rewards that are the equal of those provided by larger ventures. I have operated a professional practice of my own for many years and am now fully self-employed in this manner. It is a very satisfying thing to do.

In about two-thirds of the cases I have studied these professional or sales practitioners do not have any strong entrepreneurial pattern. Given the lack of commitment to growth, that is not surprising. These small firms do not require a pattern for their existence. That is what makes them attractive to people who desire certain aspects of entrepreneurship, but lack substantial entrepreneurial talent.

The cases of Robert Caldwell and Sherill Sutton that follow illustrate how professionals without strong patterns operate their practices.

Robert Caldwell of RW Caldwell Associates

RW Caldwell Associates is really mostly Robert Caldwell. There are part-time professionals and full-time clerical assistants, but the firm has never had more than four people working for it. Nevertheless, it provides Caldwell with a comfortable living and an opportunity to do what he enjoys.

The firm offers outplacement services to individuals and groups who are sponsored by their former employers. It makes available training in the job search process including assistance in writing resumés, interview skills development, resources for locating hidden job markets, and administrative support during a job search. The latter may include the provision of office space from which to conduct a search. Payments for the service are made by the relatively larger companies in the Western New York area that are the firm's clients. Many of these companies have been reducing force for a number of years. Most of the business is outplacement of individuals, but a small percentage stems from the conduct of group workshops. There are also opportunities in preretirement counseling and the placement of spouses who relocate to the Buffalo area business community. There is national level competition in the area, but RW Caldwell Associates has something of an advantage in that it is a locally owned and operated business with considerable experience in the proximate business community.

Caldwell has a master's degree in industrial and labor relations and was employed for many years by Bethlehem Steel Corporation, primarily in the human resource area. He started in labor relations and worked his way up to manage human resources in the huge Lackawanna plant. As that plant subsequently shut down, he handled outplacement for the company. His firm represents an extension of what he did at Bethlehem on the company side. He is by training and by long experience a human resource professional.

Insofar as the entrepreneurial patterns are concerned, Caldwell does not exhibit any to a marked degree. He is first and foremost a professional, who has established a small company to house his professional practice. Nevertheless he does possess certain strengths that aid him in his work. His achievement drive is strong; consequently he is ambitious and takes considerable pride in his accomplishments. Knowing how well he is doing is important to him and he believes that what he does, not the actions of powerful people or the luck of the draw, determines how things will turn out. He works hard at his profession, is personally committed to it, and believes in its ethical principles. Contributing to the welfare of society and of other people is important to him. In his relations with others he is warm, supportive, sensitive, and a good listener. Other people's problems are his problems. He is a very intelligent person who can indeed figure out ways of assisting those who have lost their jobs. Yet he is not a risk taker. His approach tends first and foremost to be a conservative one. Only when he is quite sure of what will work in a particular situation will he proceed.

These characteristics have stood Caldwell in good stead over the years. Over a seven-year period he has helped more than 400 people from 70 different companies. They range from hourly employees to chief executive officers. He does find jobs for them, and he knows how to introduce his clients to new careers. Furthermore, he tends to place people in positions where they stay and prosper; that is where his conservatism pays off. He does not recommend that his clients jump at the first opportunity, only at the right opportunity.

Sherill Sutton of Sassy Graphics, Inc.

Sutton is a graphic designer with a degree in textile design from Buffalo State College. Sassy Graphics, Inc., is the vehicle for her design activities. Prior to starting the company she worked at her profession, learning on the job, with two printing firms. However, she found that rather confining and now would not consider working for someone else.

Sassy Graphics is a graphic design studio that produces brochures, newsletters, letterhead, logo designs, catalogs, menus, annual reports, even books. Services include creative/concepting, layout, typesetting, mechanicals, copywriting, illustration, photography, and desktop publishing. The work is split about equally between art service, which is done on a project basis in-house, and resale, which is largely printing purchased from outside sources. Clients are heavily concentrated in various membership and professional organizations, but extend to education, tourism, retail, business-to-business, and manufacturing.

The studio has operated with from two to four employees throughout its existence. Annual sales are under $.5 million. By most business standards it has not been very profitable, but it has provided its owner with a reasonable income and security over the years. Sutton, in combination with various groups of partners, has started several other small businesses aimed at promoting various products that display her designs. The only one now operating is a signature retail store in a ski area, which sells sportswear and gift items with her original designs imprinted or embroidered on them.

Sutton is not particularly high on any of the psychological patterns, but she shows some positive strengths within all four. She is firmly convinced that she controls her own destiny. Time pressures and deadlines drive her to the point where she is somewhat stressed out. She is a self-starter who shows evidence of considerable initiative. Other people are important to her, she is very much aware of their feelings, and disagreements with them tend to bother her. All this does not quite add up to a Supersalesperson, but some of the qualities are present. Her managerial characteristics include considerable self-confidence, competitiveness, and decisiveness. She is creative and likes to try new things.

However, it is in the area of professional motivation that Sutton exhibits the most pronounced characteristics. She is strongly committed to her work and identifies with her profession as a creative artist and designer. She does other things, but this is really what she is. Also she is very independent, with the result that she sticks by her own ideas and conceptualizations. That is why she no longer wants to work with a partner or for anyone but herself either.

Sassy Graphics will do roughly 800 jobs in a year, and Sutton works with many of these clients to produce creative solutions to their needs. That is what she enjoys. There is an obvious sales/service requirement and she does her best to rise to that. In terms of promotion, she will provide a portfolio of her more creative work, showing examples to clients of what she can do for them. Cold-call sales for her company are not much fun, and she rarely does them. She can be very creative, however, in thinking up new ways to promote the studio. To really grow the organization, it would be necessary to hire people to handle marketing, finances, administration, and the like, but then it would be necessary to devote one's energies to managing these people to see that they are doing their work correctly. In the past, many did not seem to, and that produced all kinds of problems. Because all this is not particularly attractive to her, Sutton stays small enough, trying to delegate what she can, while leaving ample time to do the creative design work for clients that she loves.

PRACTICES WITH STRONG PATTERNS

RW Caldwell Associates and Sassy Graphics provide good examples of the kind of practices possible if you do not have any strong pattern. However, be aware that some practices are started and operated by people who do possess strong patterns; they may even be complex entrepreneurs, although that is not common. These practices are much like those created by Robert Caldwell and Sherry Sutton. There do not appear to be any major differences.

What is different, however, is that these firms could very well grow successfully. In my experience they do not because the private practitioner has made a calculated decision that net income is best maximized by staying small and keeping costs low. Funding growth might prove more lucrative in the long run, but it would eat into profits in the short run. At least for the present, these practitioners with strong patterns do not view this as an attractive trade-off.

The example of Steven Goodwin of Goodwin Insurance Associates illustrates a private practitioner—in this case a sales practitioner—who has strong patterns. Goodwin, in fact, has two strong patterns and thus meets the requirement for complexity.

Steven Goodwin of Goodwin Insurance Associates

Goodwin Insurance is Goodwin himself backed up by several people who provide secretarial and bookkeeping support. The company is an insurance specialty firm offering employee benefits, life, health, and disability insurance for individuals, corporations, and nonprofit organizations. It does business insurance planning, provides group insurance benefits, gets into estate planning, and also into retirement planning. The largest share of its income derives from life insurance sales. The client list is diverse but contains a goodly proportion of professionals including attorneys, physicians, and physical therapists. The company is housed in a building in downtown Buffalo that was completely renovated after Goodwin purchased it. Part of the space is rented out.

After graduating from college with a major in mass communications, Goodwin went into the family business running a shoe store. Subsequently he worked for a number of years as an insurance agent and broker for John Hancock Mutual Life, before starting his own firm. Much of the insurance he sells is still a John Hancock product.

In a business entirely devoted to sales, it is not surprising that

Goodwin has a strong dose of the Supersalesperson in his makeup. He also has a lot of the Real Manager in him, thus providing something of a hard-sell backup to his more typical soft-sell approach. He is basically a warm and sensitive person who is concerned about others and enjoys working with teams to accomplish mutual goals. Feelings are important to him—his own and those of others. He can be very persuasive, but his efforts are often devoted to helping others. He likes to protect and assist people and views insurance as a way of doing this. It is important to him that his work provide an opportunity to meet and interact with people, a sense of being valued as a person, and recognition for his accomplishments from others.

Goodwin is comfortable working with individuals who hold positions of leadership and responsibility. At the same time he also enjoys taking on a leadership role himself. He can take charge of a situation, and reaches decisions both quickly and easily. Convincing people to do things in a face-to-face setting is a major strength. Not surprisingly, he is quite effective at making presentations to groups and thoroughly enjoys doing this.

As a company Goodwin Insurance has grown steadily in terms of both the amount of insurance in effect and the dollar value of gross commissions. It is a sole proprietor sales practice. The growth has come by bidding for bigger contracts, particularly in the small business arena, and thus increasing Goodwin's own personal productivity. This is what he wants to do, not to grow a large organization. He enjoys learning about businesses and their problems and helping them grow. He spends the majority of his time doing this and is very effective in gaining the confidence of the business leaders with whom he works.

It is not uncommon for him to establish a team of lawyers, accountants, and other experts to deal with the financial planning needs of a particular client. He also has appointed a client advisory board. Through networks of alumni, organizations, religious groups, and community service providers—many of which he serves in a leadership capacity—he gets to know a large number of people. He listens to them, learns from them, and often can help to solve one of their problems by selling them some of his insurance products. As the business grows, Goodwin's days get longer and longer, but he loves spending time with people and that makes the hard work worthwhile. He has considered taking in a partner to reduce the demands on his time, but to date that has not happened. It can get a bit lonely working as he does, and when the stress builds a partner would be nice to share it with. But the satisfactions of helping others, and being constantly with other people, outweigh these difficulties.

ARE PROFESSIONAL AND SALES PRACTITIONERS ENTREPRENEURS?

If you lack any strong pattern and should decide to create a professional or sales practice, would it be appropriate to consider yourself an entrepreneur? I think not. Increasingly the idea of entrepreneurship has become aligned with either the fact of, or the intention to, build an enterprise or grow an organization.[2] A major aspect of the entrepreneur is some kind of growth orientation that leads in the case of successful applications to employment of a number of other people, and thus the need to meet a payroll.

Most individuals that I know who are self employed and have strong patterns have this growth orientation. There are exceptions; as I noted in the last section, but that is not the norm. When this growth orientation is not present designations such as private practitioner seem more appropriate. The term entrepreneur should be reserved for those cases where growth is a major goal, or at least was a major goal at some point.

CONCLUSION

I believe professional and sales practices do represent a meaningful solution for many of you who want self-employment, but lack the strong patterns of an entrepreneur. However, for such a practice to survive you must possess some special skill—either a profession, or craft, or the capacity to sell something well. This almost invariably means a certain level of education and training, either in a formal degree program, or a nondegree program, or perhaps derived from some special on-the-job learning experience.

Realistically, there are some people who are not cut out to be entrepreneurs, or private practitioners either. That is true of any occupation I know of—some people have what it takes and some do not. Luckily the world of employment is sufficiently diverse so that there is something for almost everybody. However, for those of you who have the talent for entrepreneurship, I urge you to use it as effectively as you possibly can. In a time of declining large corporations, the country needs your talents now more than it has in almost a hundred years.

NOTES

1. A study I did with Donald P. Crane and Robert J. Vandenberg that was published in *Organization Science* and that focused on labor arbitrators—most of whom were trained as lawyers—makes this point well. Almost 50 percent of these arbitrators work entirely in independent private practice, and their dominant motives are those of a professional nature.
2. Examples are the discussions by Jeffry A. Timmons in his book New *Venture Creation* and by Donald L. Sexton and Nancy B. Bowman-Upton in their book *Entrepreneurship: Creativity and Growth.*

APPENDIX A

Our Research on Entrepreneurship

For 20 years various research teams with which I have been involved have contributed to our understanding of what it takes to be a successful entrepreneur. We have had our failures, but we now know a great deal more than we knew at the beginning. The chronology of our learning is depicted in Exhibit A1. There I set forth the three phases of the research and the names of the team members in each phase. These team members did not necessarily all work together as a group. However, they did combine into various subgroups to work on particular projects together—in units of two, three, or four.

The Phase I research is best described as exploratory and not very successful. We thought that entrepreneurs might be people who grew businesses in order to have something to manage; the idea is that entrepreneurs are essentially a group of managers who take a special approach to attaining managerial jobs. This is for the most part not the case, except for some Real Manager entrepreneurs. Toward the end of this period we began to see some of the ways entrepreneurs and managers clearly do differ.

In Phase II we built on this knowledge. Our first breakthrough came with the development of a sentence completion questionnaire (MSCS—T) intended to tell us about entrepreneurial personalities.[1] It has done that, contributing substantially to our understanding of two of the four personality types—Personal Achievers and Expert Idea Generators. The questionnaire gives us insights into the role that achievement striving plays in the success of entrepreneurs and into the way that innovative ideas and risk-taking operate. We obtained completed questionnaires from hundreds of entrepreneurs all over the world. Our first group consisted of a number of

Exhibit A1   PHASES OF OUR ENTREPRENEURSHIP RESEARCH PROGRAM

Time Line

1975	1980	1985	1990	1995

Phase I

Focus on the managerial characteristics of entrepreneurs

Team members: Smith, Miner, McCain, Berman, Oliver

- Comparison of Oregon entrepreneurs with first- and mid-level managers
  - Comparison of entrepreneurs and top managers
  - Development of organization measures (including managerial and entrepreneurial)

Phase II

Focus on aspects of the Personal Achiever and Expert Idea Generator entrepreneurs

Team members: Smith, Miner, Bracker, Jourdan, Pearson, Keats, O'del, Bellu, Goldfarb, Davidsson, Porter, Sherman

- Development of an entrepreneurial personality measure (with the assistance of Oregon entrepreneurs)
  - Comparison of high technology entrepreneurs and small business managers (follow-up extending over six years)
    - Comparison of bankrupt and successful entrepreneurs in Atlanta
      - Study of planning practices among electronics entrepreneurs
      - Comparison of entrepreneurs and managers (Vermont and New York City)
        - Comparison of Canadian and U.S. students (all in entrepreneurship courses)
        - Comparison of entrepreneurs and managers (Italy, Israel, and Sweden)
          - Comparison of small-scale entrepreneurs (Poland and U.S.)

- Comparison of female entrepreneurs and managers (New York City)
  - Study of a high-growth entrepreneurial firm
  - Follow-up of entrepreneurs in a skills development workshop over five years

Phase III

Bringing the four patterns together

Team members: Miner, O'del, Newcomb, Chen, Stites-Doe, Williams, Pastor

- Study of 100 established Buffalo entrepreneurs (follow-up extending over seven years)
  - Study of graduate entrepreneurship students (follow-up extending over six years)

The Cast of Team Members (in order of their appearance)

Norman R. Smith at the University of Oregon

John B. Miner at Georgia State University and State University of New York at Buffalo

Kenneth G. McCain at University of Oregon and Boise State University

Frederic E. Berman at Georgia State University and the Berman Consulting Group

John E. Oliver at Georgia State University and Valdosta State University

Jeffrey S. Bracker at Georgia State University and Arizona State University

Louis F. Jourdan at Georgia State University

John N. Pearson at Arizona State University

Barbara W. Keats at Arizona State University

John N. O'del at State University of New York at Buffalo

Renato R. Bellu at Kingsborough College of the City University of New York

Connie Goldfarb at Kingsborough College of the City University of New York

Per Davidsson at Stockholm School of Economics, Sweden

Charles G. Porter at State University of New York at Buffalo

Carol L. Newcomb at State University of New York at Buffalo

Chao-Chuan Chen at State University of New York at Buffalo and Rutgers University

Susan Stites-Doe at State University of New York at Buffalo

Eric Williams at State University of New York at Buffalo and University of North Carolina

Juan Carlos Pastor at State University of New York at Buffalo

Herbert Sherman at Marist College

successful entrepreneurs in the state of Oregon, who actually helped us in selecting the questions to be included in the questionnaire.

From there we moved to a study of high technology entrepreneurs throughout the United States who had applied for financial assistance from the National Science Foundation. More than half of these people hold Ph.D. degrees and almost all have advanced degrees beyond college. Yet that did not appear to make them successful entrepreneurs necessarily; some are, but a number had firms that did not survive very long. We followed these people using letters and phone calls over almost six years. We learned a lot from them about the kinds of entrepreneurs that achieve success and those that do not. A number turned out to be professional practitioners.

Many studies using the entrepreneurial personality questionnaire focus on specific groups at a point in time, often comparing individuals who start businesses of their own with managers who do not. This approach was used in the state of Vermont and in the New York City area with males, and in New York City only with females. A study in Atlanta, starting from court records of bankruptcy, compared entrepreneurs who fail with those whose businesses survive. Administering our questionnaire along with a survey of planning activities to entrepreneurs in the electronics industry gave us considerable understanding of the importance of planning in firm success.

Then there are the international studies, which attempt to determine whether what we learned about entrepreneurial personalities in the United States has wider application. In certain instances we find that it does. That clearly is the case in Italy and in Israel. However, in Sweden and post-communist Poland there are departures from the U.S. patterns.

These studies with the MSCS—T personality questionnaire are useful in that they permit comparisons of various groups using the same measure.[2] The problem is that we do not get to know the entrepreneurs very well. Too much of what we learn is obtained at arm's length. Beginning in 1987, however, that began to change. At that time a development program for established entrepreneurs in the Buffalo area was introduced by the State University. I was involved in the start-up of that venture, and thus began Phase III. A total of 100 established entrepreneurs were studied. Phase III also included a study of 150 students in my graduate entrepreneurship course at the State University of New York at Buffalo. This book's Introduction describes the Phase III research.

The Phase III research as a whole led to the development of the four patterns described in this book, the idea of appropriate career routes that fit with each pattern, and the concept of a complex entrepreneur. I feel that we finally have at least the core understanding necessary to predict who will and will not be a successful entrepreneur.

NOTES

1. This is Form T of the Miner Sentence Completion Scale. I describe it in my *Scoring Guide for the Miner Sentence Completion Scale—Form T* (1986).
2. These studies are written up and in most cases published. The citations are contained in the reference section that follows these appendixes. The authors are among the team members noted in Exhibit A1. The 27 publications available to date are marked with an asterisk in the References. The most comprehensive review of this material is in my book *Role Motivation Theories* (1993).

APPENDIX B

Measuring the Entrepreneurial Patterns

On the Self Assessment Form in Chapter 10, there are standards that determine whether a person's score qualifies that person as a Personal Achiever, Supersalesperson, Real Manager, or Expert Idea Generator. These standards are based on the 100 established entrepreneurs I studied, and the test measures used to establish these standards are the subject of this appendix.

Listed below is each characteristic for each entrepreneurial pattern, followed by the test measures used to identify the characteristic, and the literature that references that measure. (Measures marked with an asterisk were originally included in the test battery because they are short, easily scored, and thus useful for teaching people to understand the characteristic.)

For each test measure, I converted the results into the three-point scale (0, 1, or 2) discussed in Chapter 10. For each entrepreneurial pattern, these converted scores were first averaged to obtain scores for the characteristic, and then the characteristic scores were totaled. The standards in Chapter 10 derive from the distributions of these total pattern scores.

Personal Achiever Entrepreneur

1. *Need to Achieve*
   Miner Sentence Completion Scale—Form T: Self Achievement
   Miner, John B. *Scoring Guide for the Miner Sentence Completion Scale—Form T (MSCS—T).*
   Miner, John B. *Role Motivation Theories.*

Test scores of—		Pattern scores of—
–8 to +1	=	0
+2 and +3	=	1
+4 to +8	=	2

*Lynn Achievement Motivation Questionnaire
Hines, George H., writing in the *Journal of Applied Psychology*.
Lynn, Richard, writing in the *British Journal of Psychology*.

Test scores of—		Pattern scores of—
0 to 5	=	0
6 and 7	=	1
8	=	2

*Individual Behavior Activity Profile (abbreviated)
Matteson, Michael T., and John M. Ivancevich. *Managing Job Stress and Health*.
Matteson, Michael T., and John M. Ivancevich, writing in the *Journal of Occupational Medicine*.

Test scores of—		Pattern scores of—
0 to 44	=	0
45 to 59	=	1
60 to 75	=	2

*Rose Tension Discharge Rate Scale
Matteson, Michael T., and John M. Ivancevich, writing in the *Academy of Management Journal*.
Rose, R. M., C. D. Jenkins, and M. W. Hurst. *Air Traffic Controller Health Change Study*.

Test scores of—		Pattern scores of—
6 to 24	=	0
25 to 30	=	1
31 to 42	=	2

2. *Desire for Feedback*
   Miner Sentence Completion Scale—Form T: Feedback of Results
   Miner, John B. *Scoring Guide for the MSCS—T*.
   Miner, John B. *Role Motivation Theories*.

Test scores of—		Pattern scores of—
−8 to −1	=	0
0 to +1	=	1
+2 to +8	=	2

3. *Desire to Plan and Set Goals*
   Miner Sentence Completion Scale—Form T: Planning for the Future
   Miner, John B. *Scoring Guide for the MSCS—T*.
   Miner, John B. *Role Motivation Theories*.

Test scores of—		Pattern scores of—
−8 to 0	=	0
+1 and +2	=	1
+3 to +8	=	2

4. *Strong Personal Initiative*
   Ghiselli Self-Description Inventory: Initiative
   Ghiselli, Edwin E. *Explorations in Managerial Talent.*

Test scores of—		Pattern scores of—
0 to 37	=	0
38 to 40	=	1
41 to 47	=	2

5. *Strong Personal Commitment to Their Organization*
   Miner Sentence Completion Scale—Form P: Professional Commitment
   Miner, John B. *Scoring Guide for the Miner Sentence Completion Scale—Form P (MSCS—P).*
   Miner, John B. *Role Motivation Theories.*

Test scores of—		Pattern scores of—
−8 to +1	=	0
+2 and +3	=	1
+4 to +8	=	2

   Miner Sentence Completion Scale—Form P: Acquiring Knowledge
   Miner, John B. *Scoring Guide for the MSCS—P.*
   Miner, John B. *Role Motivation Theories.*

Test scores of—		Pattern scores of—
−8 to +1	=	0
+2 and +3	=	1
+4 to +8	=	2

6. *Belief That One Person Can Make a Difference*
   *Matteson and Ivancevich Internal-External Scale
   Matteson, Michael T., and John M. Ivancevich. *Managing Job Stress and Health.*

Test scores of—		Pattern scores of—
5 to 8	=	0
3 and 4	=	1
0 to 2	=	2

   Levenson Internal-External Instrument: I (Internal) Scale
   Levenson, Hanna, writing in the *Journal of Personality Assessment.*
   Levenson, Hanna, writing in the *Proceedings of the American Psychological Association.*

Test scores of—		Pattern scores of—
8 to 39	=	0
40 to 42	=	1
43 to 48	=	2

Levenson Internal-External Instrument: P (Powerful Others) Scale
Levenson, Hanna, writing in the *Journal of Personality Assessment.*
Levenson, Hanna, writing in the *Proceedings of the American Psychological Association.*

Test scores of—		Pattern scores of—
18 to 48	=	0
14 to 17	=	1
8 to 13	=	2

Levenson Internal-External Instrument: C (Chance) Scale
Levenson, Hanna, writing in the *Journal of Personality Assessment.*
Levenson, Hanna, writing in the *Proceedings of the American Psychological Association.*

Test scores of—		Pattern scores of—
16 to 48	=	0
13 to 15	=	1
8 to 12	=	2

7. *Belief That Work Should Be Guided by Personal Goals, Not Those of Others*
Oliver Organization Description Questionnaire: T Score (completed for an ideal work situation)
Oliver, John E., writing in the *Academy of Management Journal.*
Oliver, John E. *Scoring Guide for the Oliver Organization Description Questionnaire (OODQ).*
Miner, John B. *Role Motivation Theories.*

Test scores of—		Pattern scores of—
0 to 4	=	0
5 to 9	=	1
10 to 15	=	2

Oliver Organization Description Questionnaire: G Score (completed for an ideal work situation)
Oliver, John E., writing in the *Academy of Management Journal.*
Oliver, John E. *Scoring Guide for the OODQ.*
Miner, John B. *Role Motivation Theories.*

Test scores of—		Pattern scores of—
5 to 15	=	0
2 to 4	=	1
0 and 1	=	2

Supersalesperson Entrepreneur

1. *Capacity to Understand and Feel with Another*
Problem-Solving Questionnaire: Feeling

Slocum, John W., and Don Hellriegel, writing in *Business Horizons*.

Test scores of—		Pattern scores of—
0 to 3	=	0
4 and 5	=	1
6 to 8	=	2

Decision Style Inventory: Behavioral

Rowe, Alan J., and Richard O. Mason. *Managing with Style.*

Test scores of—		Pattern scores of—
20 to 61	=	0
62 to 69	=	1
70 to 160	=	2

2. *Desire to Help Others*

Miner Sentence Completion Scale—Form P: Providing Help

Miner, John B. *Scoring Guide for the MSCS—P.*

Miner, John B. *Role Motivation Theories.*

Test scores of—		Pattern scores of—
−8 to +3	=	0
+4	=	1
+5 to +8	=	2

3. *Belief That Social Processes Are Very Important*

Elizur Work Values Questionnaire: nos. 5, 7, 8, 18 and 20 of the 24-item measure

Elizur, Dov, writing in the *Journal of Applied Psychology.*

Meindl, James R., Raymond G. Hunt, and Wonsick Lee, writing in *Research in Personnel and Human Resources Management.*

Test scores of—		Pattern scores of—
10 to 30	=	0
8 and 9	=	1
5 to 7	=	2

4. *Need to Have Strong Positive Relationships with Others*

The Least Preferred Coworker (LPC) Scale

Fiedler, Fred E., and Martin M. Chemers. *Improving Leadership Effectiveness.*

Test scores of—		Pattern scores of—
18 to 64	=	0
65 to 72	=	1
73 to 144	=	2

5. *Belief That a Sales Force Is Crucial to Carrying Out Company Strategy*

Company Survey: Ranking of Competitive Strategies

Smith, Norman R. *The Entrepreneur and His Firm.*
Miner, John B., Norman R. Smith, and Jeffrey S. Bracker, writing in the *Journal of Business Venturing.*

		Pattern scores of—
Sales force not ranked in top six	=	0
Sales force ranked 4 to 6	=	1
Sales force ranked 1 to 3	=	2

Real Manager Entrepreneur

1. *Desire to Be a Corporate Leader*
   Ghiselli Self-Description Inventory: Supervisory Ability
   Ghiselli, Edwin E. *Explorations in Managerial Talent.*

Test scores of—		Pattern scores of—
0 to 36	=	0
37 to 39	=	1
40 to 47	=	2

   Ghiselli Self-Description Inventory: Self-Assurance
   Ghiselli, Edwin E. *Explorations in Managerial Talent.*

Test scores of—		Pattern scores of—
0 to 32	=	0
33 to 35	=	1
36 to 41	=	2

   Ghiselli Self-Description Inventory: The Need for Occupational Achievement
   Ghiselli, Edwin E. *Explorations in Managerial Talent.*

Test scores of—		Pattern scores of—
0 to 49	=	0
50 to 53	=	1
54 to 62	=	2

   Ghiselli Self-Description Inventory: Need for Self-Actualization
   Ghiselli, Edwin E. *Explorations in Managerial Talent.*

Test scores of—		Pattern scores of—
0 to 13	=	0
14 and 15	=	1
16 to 18	=	2

   Ghiselli Self-Description Inventory: Need for Job Security
   Ghiselli, Edwin E. *Explorations in Managerial Talent.*

Test scores of—		Pattern scores of—
9 to 19	=	0
7 and 8	=	1
0 to 6	=	2

2. *Decisiveness*
   Ghiselli Self-Description Inventory: Decisiveness
   Ghiselli, Edwin E. *Explorations in Managerial Talent.*

Test scores of—		Pattern scores of—
0 to 26	=	0
27 to 29	=	1
30 to 32	=	2

3. *Positive Attitudes to Authority*
   Miner Sentence Completion Scale—Form H: Authority Figures
   Miner, John B. *Scoring Guide for the Miner Sentence Completion Scale—Form H (MSCS—H).*
   Miner, John B. *Role Motivation Theories.*

Test scores of—		Pattern scores of—
−5 to +1	=	0
+2	=	1
+3 to +5	=	2

4. *Desire to Compete*
   Miner Sentence Completion Scale—Form H: Competitive Situations
   Miner, John B. *Scoring Guide for the MSCS—H.*
   Miner, John B. *Role Motivation Theories.*

Test scores of—		Pattern scores of—
−5 to 0	=	0
+1	=	1
+2 to +5	=	2

   Miner Sentence Completion Scale—Form H: Competitive Games
   Miner, John B. *Scoring Guide for the MSCS—H.*
   Miner, John B. *Role Motivation Theories.*

Test scores of—		Pattern scores of—
−5 to +2	=	0
+3	=	1
+4 and +5	=	2

   Miner Sentence Completion Scale—Form H: Assertive Role (Masculine Role)
   Miner, John B. *Scoring Guide for the MSCS—H.*
   Miner, John B. *Role Motivation Theories.*

Test scores of—		Pattern scores of—
−5 to +1	=	0
+2	=	1
+3 to +5	=	2

5. *Desire for Power*
   Miner Sentence Completion Scale—Form H: Imposing Wishes
   Miner, John B. *Scoring Guide for the MSCS—H.*
   Miner, John B. *Role Motivation Theories.*

Test scores of—		Pattern scores of—
−5 to +1	=	0
+2	=	1
+3 to +5	=	2

Decision Style Inventory: Directive
Rowe, Alan J., and Richard O. Mason. *Managing with Style.*

Test scores of—		Pattern scores of—
20 to 81	=	0
82 to 89	=	1
90 to 160	=	2

6. *Desire to Stand Out from the Crowd*
   Miner Sentence Completion Scale—Form H: Standing Out from Group
   Miner, John B. *Scoring Guide for the MSCS—H.*
   Miner, John B. *Role Motivation Theories.*

Test scores of—		Pattern scores of—
−5 to +1	=	0
+2	=	1
+3 to +5	=	2

Miner Sentence Completion Scale—Form H: Routine Administrative
Functions
Miner, John B. *Scoring Guide for the MSCS—H.*
Miner, John B. *Role Motivation Theories.*

Test scores of—		Pattern scores of—
−5 to +1	=	0
+2	=	1
+3 to +5	=	2

Expert Idea Generator Entrepreneur

1. *Desire to Innovate*
   Miner Sentence Completion Scale—Form T: Personal Innovation

Miner, John B. *Scoring Guide for the MSCS—T.*
Miner, John B. *Role Motivation Theories.*

Test scores of—		Pattern scores of—
−8 to +2	=	0
+3 and +4	=	1
+5 to +8	=	2

2. *Love of Ideas*
   Problem-Solving Questionnaire: Intuition
   Slocum, John W., and Don Hellriegel, writing in *Business Horizons.*

Test scores of—		Pattern scores of—
0 to 4	=	0
5 and 6	=	1
7 and 8	=	2

   Decision Style Inventory: Conceptual
   Rowe, Alan J., and Richard O. Mason. *Managing with Style.*

Test scores of—		Pattern scores of—
20 to 86	=	0
87 to 94	=	1
95 to 160	=	2

3. *Belief That New Product Development Is Crucial to Carrying Out Company Strategy*
   Company Survey: Ranking of Competitive Strategies
   Smith, Norman R. *The Entrepreneur and His Firm.*
   Miner, John B., Norman R. Smith, and Jeffrey S. Bracker, writing in
   the *Journal of Business Venturing.*

		Pattern scores of—
New product development not ranked in top six	=	0
New product development ranked 4 to 6	=	1
New product development ranked 1 to 3	=	2

4. *Good Intelligence*
   Ghiselli Self-Description Inventory: Intelligence
   Ghiselli, Edwin E. *Explorations in Managerial Talent.*

Test scores of—		Pattern scores of—
0 to 48	=	0
49 to 51	=	1
52 to 57	=	2

Vocabulary Test G-T

Thorndike, Robert L., and George H. Gallup, writing in the *Journal of General Psychology.*

Miner, John B. *Intelligence in the United States.*

Test scores (Forms A&B)—		Pattern scores of—
0 to 28	=	0
29 to 33	=	1
34 to 40	=	2

5. *Desire to Avoid Taking Risks*

Miner Sentence Completion Scale—Form T: Avoiding Risks

Miner, John B. *Scoring Guide for the MSCS—T.*

Miner, John B. *Role Motivation Theories.*

Test scores of—		Pattern scores of—
–8 to 0	=	0
+1 to +2	=	1
+3 to +8	=	2

*Shure and Meeker Risk Avoidance Scale

Shure, G. H., and J. P. Meeker, writing in the *Journal of Psychology.*

Harnett, Donald L., and Larry L. Cummings. *Bargaining Behavior.*

Test scores of—		Pattern scores of—
17 to 36	=	0
37 to 40	=	1
41 to 51	=	2

References

All publications mentioned in the chapter-end Notes and in the Appendixes are fully cited here. Publications preceded by an asterisk (*) describe parts of our entrepreneurship research program.

Atkinson, John W., and Joel O. Raynor. *Motivation and Achievement*. New York: Wiley, 1974.

Baldwin, Timothy T., and Margaret Y. Padgett. Management Development: A Review and Commentary. *International Review of Industrial and Organizational Psychology*, 8 (1993), 35–85.

*Bellu, Renato R. Entrepreneurs and Managers: Are They Different? *Frontiers of Entrepreneurship Research* (pp. 16–30). Babson Park, Mass.: Babson College, 1988.

*Bellu, Renato R. Toward a Theory of Entrepreneurial Motivation: Evidence from Female Entrepreneurs. *International Council for Small Business Proceedings*, 37 (1992), 195–213.

*Bellu, Renato R. Task Role Motivation and Attributional Style as Predictors of Entrepreneurial Performance: Female Sample Findings. *Entrepreneurship and Regional Development*, 5, no. 4 (Oct.–Dec. 1993), 331–344.

*Bellu, Renato R., Per Davidsson, and Connie Goldfarb. Motivational Characteristics of Small Firm Entrepreneurs in Israel, Italy, and Sweden: A Cross Cultural Study. *International Council for Small Business Proceedings*, 34 (1989), 349–364.

*Bellu, Renato R., Per Davidsson, and Connie Goldfarb. Toward a Theory of Entrepreneurial Behavior: Empiricial Evidence from Israel, Italy, and Sweden. *Entrepreneurship and Regional Development*, 2, no. 2 (Apr.–June 1990), 195–209.

*Bellu, Renato R., and Herbert Sherman. Predicting Entrepreneurial Success from Task Motivation and Attributional Style: A Longitudinal Study. *Proceedings of the United States Association for Small Business and Entrepreneurship*, 8 (1993), 16–23.

*Bellu, Renato R., and Herbert Sherman. Predicting Firm Success from Task Motivation and Attributional Style: A Longitudinal Study. *Entrepreneurship and Regional Development*, 7, no. 4 (Oct.-Dec. 1995), 349–363.

*Berman, Frederic E., and John B. Miner. Motivation to Manage at the Top Executive Level: A Test of the Hierarchic Role-Motivation Theory. *Personnel Psychology*, 38, no. 2 (Summer 1985), 377–391.

Bird, Barbara J. *Entrepreneurial Behavior.* Glenview, Ill.: Scott, Foresman, 1989.

Block, Zenas, and Ian C. MacMillan. *Corporate Venturing: Creating New Businesses Within the Firm.* Boston: Harvard Business School Press, 1993.

Boyd, Brian K. Strategic Planning and Financial Performance: A Meta-Analytic Review. *Journal of Management Studies*, 28, no. 4 (July 1991), 353–374.

*Bracker, Jeffrey S., John N. Pearson, Barbara W. Keats, and John B. Miner. Entrepreneurial Intensity, Strategic Planning Process Sophistication, and Firm Performance in a Dynamic Environment. Abstracted in John B. Miner, *Role Motivation Theories* (pp. 155–156). New York: Routledge, 1993.

Brockhaus, Robert H. Risk Taking Propensity of Entrepreneurs. *Academy of Management Journal*, 23, no. 3 (Sept. 1980), 509–520.

Burgelman, Robert A., and Leonard R. Sayles. *Inside Corporate Innovation: Strategy, Structure, and Managerial Skills.* New York: Free Press, 1986.

Churchill, Neil C., and Virginia L. Lewis. The Five Stages of Small Business Growth. *Harvard Business Review*, 61, no. 3 (May–June 1983), 30–50.

Collins, Orvis F., and David G. Moore. *The Enterprising Man.* East Lansing: Bureau of Business and Economic Research, Graduate School of Business Administration, Michigan State University, 1964.

Cornwall, Jeffrey R., and Baron Perlman. *Organizational Entrepreneurship.* Homewood, Ill.: Irwin, 1990.

Dyer, W. Gibb. *The Entrepreneurial Experience: Confronting Career Dilemmas of the Start-up Executive.* San Francisco: Jossey-Bass, 1992.

Ehringer, Ann G. *Make Up Your Mind: Entrepreneurs Talk About Decision Making.* Santa Monica, Calif.: Merritt, 1995.

Elizur, Dov. Facets of Work Values: A Structural Analysis of Work Outcomes. *Journal of Applied Psychology*, 69, no. 3 (Aug. 1984), 379–389.

Fiedler, Fred E., and Martin M. Chemers. *Improving Leadership Effectiveness: The Leader Match Concept.* New York: Wiley, 1984.

Fiedler, Fred E., and Joseph E. Garcia. *New Approaches to Effective Leadership: Cognitive Resources and Organizational Performance.* New York: Wiley, 1987.

Galbraith, Jay. New Venture Planning—The Stages of Growth. *Journal of Business Strategy*, 3, no. 1 Summer 1982), 70–79.

Ghiselli, Edwin E. *Explorations in Managerial Talent*. Pacific Palisades, Calif.: Goodyear, 1971.

Hagan, Oliver, Carol Rivchun, and Donald Sexton. *Women-Owned Businesses*. New York: Praeger, 1989.

Harnett, Donald L., and Larry L. Cummings. *Bargaining Behavior: An International Study*. Houston, Tex.: Dame Publications, 1980.

Hines, George H. Achievement Motivation, Occupations, and Labor Turnover in New Zealand. *Journal of Applied Psychology*, 58, no. 3 (Dec. 1973), 313–317.

Hisrich, Robert D., and Candida G. Brush. *The Woman Entrepreneur: Starting, Financing, and Managing a Successful New Business*. Lexington, Mass.: Lexington Books, 1986.

Hisrich, Robert D., and Michael P. Peters. *Entrepreneurship: Starting, Developing, and Managing a New Enterprise*. Homewood, Ill.: Irwin, 1995.

*Jourdan, Louis F. Differentiation Between Successful and Unsuccessful Entrepreneurs. Unpublished doctoral dissertation, Georgia State University, 1987.

Kao, John J. *Entrepreneurship, Creativity, and Organization*. Englewood Cliffs, N.J.: Prentice Hall, 1995.

Katzenbach, Jon R., and Douglas K. Smith. *The Wisdom of Teams: Creating the High-Performance Organization*. Harvard Business School Press, 1993.

Levenson, Hanna. Distinctions Within the Concept of Internal-External Control: Development of a New Scale. *Proceedings of the American Psychological Association Annual Convention*, 80th Convention (1972), pp. 261–262.

Levenson, Hanna. Activism and Powerful Others: Distinctions Within the Concept of Internal-External Control. *Journal of Personality Assessment*, 38, no. 4 (Aug. 1974), 377–383.

Levinson, Harry. Why the Behemoths Fall: Psychological Roots of Corporate Failure. *American Psychologist*, 49, no. 5 (May 1994), 428–436.

Lynn, Richard. An Achievement Motivation Questionnaire. *British Journal of Psychology*, 60, no. 4 (1969), 529–534.

Matteson, Michael T., and John M. Ivancevich. *Managing Job Stress and Health: The Intelligent Person's Guide*. New York: Free Press, 1982.

Matteson, Michael T., and John M. Ivancevich. Type A and B Behavior Patterns and Self-Reported Health Symptoms and Stress: Examining Individual and Organizational Fit. *Journal of Occupational Medicine*, 24 (1982), 585–589.

Matteson, Michael T., and John M. Ivancevich. Note on Tension Discharge Rate as an Employee Health Status Predictor. *Academy of Management Journal*, 26, no. 3 (Sept. 1983), 540–545.

McCaskey, Michael B. *The Executive Challenge: Managing Change and Ambiguity.* Boston: Pitman, 1982.

McClelland, David C. *The Achieving Society.* New York: Van Nostrand, 1961.

McClelland, David C. *Power: The Inner Experience.* New York: Irvington, 1975.

McClelland, David C., and David G. Winter. *Motivating Economic Achievement.* New York: Free Press, 1969.

Meindl, James R., Raymond G. Hunt, and Wonsick Lee. Individualism-Collectivism and Work Values: Data from the United States, China, Taiwan, Korea, and Hong Kong. *Research in Personnel and Human Resources Management.* Supplement 1, 1989, pp. 59–77.

Miller, Danny. *The Icarus Paradox: How Exceptional Companies Bring About Their Own Downfall.* New York: Harper Business, 1990.

Miner, John B. *Scoring Guide for the Miner Sentence Completion Scale—Form H.* Eugene, Ore.: Organizational Measurement Systems Press, 1964. Supplements 1977, 1989.

Miner, John B. *Intelligence in the United States.* New York: Springer, 1957; reprint Greenwood Press, 1973.

Miner, John B. *Scoring Guide for the Miner Sentence Completion Scale—Form P.* Eugene, Ore.: Organizational Measurement Systems Press, 1981.

Miner, John B. *People Problems: The Executive Answer Book.* New York: Random House, 1985.

*Miner, John B. *Scoring Guide for the Miner Sentence Completion Scale—Form T.* Eugene, Ore.: Organizational Measurement Systems Press, 1986.

*Miner, John B. Entrepreneurs, High Growth Entrepreneurs, and Managers: Contrasting and Overlapping Motivational Patterns. *Journal of Business Venturing,* 5, no. 4 (July 1990), 221–234.

*Miner, John B. Individuals, Groups, and Networking: Experience with an Entrepreneurship Development Program. *International Council for Small Business Proceedings,* 36 (1991), 82–90.

*Miner, John B. *Role Motivation Theories.* New York: Routledge, 1993.

Miner, John B., and Donald P. Crane. *Human Resource Management: The Strategic Perspective.* New York: HarperCollins, 1995.

Miner, John B., Donald P. Crane, and Robert J. Vandenberg. Congruence and Fit in Professional Role Motivation Theory. *Organization Science,* 5, no. 1 (Feb. 1994), 86–97.

*Miner, John B., Norman R. Smith, and Jeffrey S. Bracker. Role of Entrepreneurial Task Motivation in the Growth of Technologically Innovative Firms. *Journal of Applied Psychology,* 74, no. 4 (Aug. 1989), 554–560.

*Miner, John B., Norman R. Smith, and Jeffrey S. Bracker. Defining the Inventor-Entrepreneur in the Context of Established Typologies. *Journal of Business Venturing,* 7, no. 2 (Mar. 1992), 103–113.

*Miner, John B., Norman R. Smith, and Jeffrey S. Bracker. Predicting Firm Survival from a Knowledge of Entrepreneur Task Motivation. *Entrepreneurship and Regional Development*, 4, no. 2 (Apr.–June 1992), 145–153.

*Miner, John B., Norman R. Smith, and Jeffrey S. Bracker. Role of Entrepreneurial Task Motivation in the Growth of Technologically Innovative Firms: Interpretations from Follow-up Data. *Journal of Applied Psychology*, 79, no. 4 (Aug. 1994), 627–630.

*Miner, John B., and Susan Stites-Doe. Applying an Entrepreneurship Development Program to Economic Problems in the Buffalo Area. In Abraham K. Korman (ed.), *Human Dilemmas in Work Organizations: Strategies for Resolution* (pp. 243–271). New York: Guilford Press, 1994.

Miron, David, and David C. McClelland. The Impact of Achievement Motivation Training on Small Business. *California Management Review*, 21, no. 4 (Summer 1979), 13–28.

Mowday, Richard T., Lyman W. Porter, and Richard M. Steers. *Employee-Organization Linkages: The Psychology of Commitment, Absenteeism, and Turnover.* New York: Academic Press, 1982.

Oakes, Guy. *The Soul of the Salesman: The Moral Ethos of Personal Sales.* Atlantic Highlands, N.J.: Humanities Press International, 1990.

*O'del, John N. A Comparative Study of Polish and American Entrepreneurs: An Analysis Using Task Role Motivation Theory. Unpublished doctoral dissertation, State University of New York at Buffalo, 1994.

*Oliver, John E. *Scoring Guide for the Oliver Organization Description Questionnaire.* Eugene, Ore.: Organizational Measurement Systems Press, 1981.

*Oliver, John E. An Instrument for Classifying Organizations. *Academy of Management Journal*, 25, no. 4 (Dec. 1982), 855–866.

Porter, Lyman W., and Lawrence E. McKibbin. *Management Education and Development: Drift or Thrust Into the 21st Century.* New York: McGraw-Hill, 1988.

Roberts, Edward B. *Entrepreneurs in High Technology: Lessons from MIT and Beyond.* New York: Oxford University Press, 1991.

Rose, R. M., C. D. Jenkins, and M. W. Hurst. *Air Traffic Controller Health Change Study: A Prospective Investigation of Physical, Psychological, and Work-Related Changes.* Austin: University of Texas Press, 1978.

Rowe, Alan J., and Richard O. Mason. *Managing with Style: A Guide to Understanding, Assessing, and Improving Decision Making.* San Francisco: Jossey-Bass, 1987.

Runco, Mark A., and Robert S. Albert. *Theories of Creativity.* Newbury Park, Calif.: Sage, 1990.

Sandberg, William R. *New Venture Performance: The Role of Strategy and Industry Structure.* Lexington, Mass.: Lexington Books, 1986.

Sexton, Donald L., and Nancy B. Bowman-Upton. *Entrepreneurship: Creativity and Growth.* New York: Macmillan, 1991.

Shefsky, Lloyd E. *Entrepreneurs Are Made Not Born.* New York: McGraw-Hill, 1994.

Shure, G. H., and J. P. Meeker. A Personality Attitude Schedule for Use in Experimental Bargaining Studies. *Journal of Psychology,* 65 (1967), 233–252.

Slocum, John W., and Don Hellriegel. A Look at How Manager's Minds Work. *Business Horizons,* 26, no. 4 (July–Aug. 1983), 58–68.

Smith, Norman R. *The Entrepreneur and His Firm: The Relationship Between Type of Man and Type of Company.* East Lansing: Bureau of Business and Economic Research, Graduate School of Business Administration, Michigan State University, 1967.

*Smith, Norman R., Jeffrey S. Bracker, and John B. Miner. Correlates of Firm and Entrepreneur Success in Technologically Innovative Companies. *Frontiers of Entrepreneurship Research* (pp. 337–353). Babson Park, Mass.: Babson College, 1987.

*Smith, Norman R., Kenneth G. McCain, and John B. Miner. The Managerial Motivation of Successful Entrepreneurs. *Oregon Business Review,* 34 (1976), 3.

*Smith, Norman R., and John B. Miner. Type of Entrepreneur, Type of Firm, and Managerial Motivation: Implications for Organizational Life Cycle Theory. *Strategic Management Journal,* 4, no. 4 (Oct.–Dec. 1983), 325–340.

*Smith, Norman R., and John B. Miner. Motivational Considerations in the Success of Technologically Innovative Entrepreneurs. *Frontiers of Entrepreneurship Research* (pp. 488–495). Babson Park, Mass.: Babson College, 1984.

*Smith, Norman R., and John B. Miner. Motivational Considerations in the Success of Technologically Innovative Entrepreneurs: Extended Sample Findings. *Frontiers of Entrepreneurship Research* (pp. 482–488). Babson Park, Mass.: Babson College, 1985.

Sonnenfeld, Jeffrey. *The Hero's Farewell: What Happens When CEOs Retire.* New York: Oxford University Press, 1988.

Stewart, Alex. *Team Entrepreneurship.* Newbury Park, Calif.: Sage, 1989.

Strube, Michael J. *Type A Behavior.* Newbury Park, Calif.: Sage, 1991.

Tannenbaum, Scott I., and Gary Yukl. Training and Development in Work Organizations. *Annual Review of Psychology,* 43 (1992), 399–441.

Taylor, Calvin W. *Climate for Creativity.* Elmsford, N.Y.: Pergamon Press, 1972.

Thorndike, Robert L., and George H. Gallup. Verbal Intelligence of the American Adult. *Journal of General Psychology,* 30 (1944), 75–85.

Timmons, Jeffry A. *The Entrepreneurial Mind*. Andover, Mass.: Brick House, 1989.

Timmons, Jeffry A. *New Venture Creation: Entrepreneurship in the 1990s*. Homewood, Ill.: Irwin, 1990.

Vesper, Karl H. *New Venture Strategies*. Englewood Cliffs, N.J.: Prentice Hall, 1990.

Wallace, Phyllis A. *MBAs on the Fast Track: Career Mobility of Young Managers*. New York: Ballinger, 1989.

Ward, J. L. *Keeping the Family Business Healthy*. San Francisco: Jossey-Bass, 1987.

Name Index

Subject Index

About the Author

J ohn B. Miner currently has a professional practice (at 34199 Country View Drive, Eugene, OR 97408) specializing in entrepreneurship and human resource management. This practice includes writing on various business subjects, consulting to both organizations and individuals, serving as an expert witness in court, and speaking to professional and business groups.

Dr. Miner received his undergraduate degree in psychology from Princeton University. After a master's degree in clinical psychology from Clark University in Worcester, Massachusetts, he returned to Princeton, where he earned his Ph.D. in personality theory and clinical psychology. While at Princeton he held the James Theodore Walker Fellowship, taught, and served as a research project director.

Subsequently Dr. Miner held research positions at Columbia University as a research associate and with the Atlantic Refining Company as Manager of Psychological Services. His career as a faculty member in business schools began at the University of Oregon, where he was appointed a full professor at the age of 35. At the University of Maryland, he was professor of both business and psychology and chaired a department. At Georgia State University, he was a research professor in three areas—business administration, industrial relations, and psychology—and also served as Doctoral Program Coordinator. At the State University of New York at Buffalo, he held the Donald S. Carmichael chair in human resources, was director of the Center for Entrepreneurial Leadership, and again chaired his department. He has held visiting professorships at the Wharton School of the University of Pennsylvania, at the University of California at Berkeley, and at the University of South Florida.

Throughout his career Dr. Miner has been active in a number of professional associations, including the Academy of Management, American Psychological Association, Society for Personality Assessment, Society for Industrial and Organizational Psychology, and American Psychological Society—all of which have awarded him the honor of Fellow status. Within the Academy of Management, his positions have included editor of the *Academy of Management Journal* and president of the Academy.

As a writer Dr. Miner has authored some 35 books dealing with topics in industrial/organizational psychology, organizational behavior, and strategic management, as well as entrepreneurship and human resource management. As a contributor to the professional and business literature, he has written well over 100 articles and book chapters. He has also authored several psychological tests.

Dr. Miner has been involved in consulting engagements for a number of organizations, both large and small. Among the former, major clients have been McKinsey & Company, Western Michigan University, AT&T, Baxter Laboratories, Southern Illinois University, and Standard Oil of Ohio. Small entrepreneurial clients include Wittreich Associates, Sterling Institute, Roundtable Films, InterGram, Perry's Ice Cream, Taylor Devices, and Elizabeth A. Clarke & Associates.

As an expert witness Dr. Miner has worked with a number of law firms, serving such companies as Rubbermaid, Georgia Kaolin, Darby Printing, Lithonia Lighting, and Georgia-Pacific. He has also had the U.S. Equal Employment Opportunity Commission as a client and served as an expert for a number of individual plaintiffs.

Dr. Miner's speaking activities include keynote or special addresses to the Southern Management Association, Advanced Management Institute, American College of Hospital Administrators, Academy of Management, Printing Industries of America, and Society for Human Resource Management. He has conducted special training sessions or workshops for, among others, Xerox, General Electric, the University of Witwatersrand, the American Psychological Association, and Arcata National Corporation.